Lys de Bray

COTTAGE GARDEN YEAR

Lys de Bray

COTTAGE GARDEN YEAR

Published by Grange Books, 1991
The Grange
Grange Yard
London SE1 3AG
England

This 1991 edition for Grange Books
is produced by Savitri Books Ltd
Southbank House
Suite 106
Black Prince Road
London SE1 7SJ

Printed and bound in Hong Kong

ISBN 1 85627 056 4

Contents

Preface 6

January 8
February 20
March 28
April 36
May 46
June 54
July 66
August 78
September 92
October 108
November 122
December 142

Index 158

Fuchsia 'Little Fellow'

Preface

When one falls in love late in life it can lead to some unexpected changes. I fell in love with a garden and that is what this book is all about.

About twelve years ago I was living alone in a little house at the edge of this small country town. The little house had only a tiny back yard, but from my bedroom windows I could see into the garden of the beautiful thatched cottage across the road. The garden was on two levels and was enclosed by old walls and fragile fences grown over with Jasmine, Lilac, Roses, Clematis, Forsythia and Mock-Orange, with tall Hollyhocks that smiled at the passers-by in the summer. I would stand and watch the garden dreaming quietly in the sunshine, and as time went on I came to know it well.

Then a miraculous thing happened. I had been very ill and was still unable to walk far, so a kind and thoughtful friend brought me a sheaf of field flowers. There were Buttercups, Ox-eye Daisies, pink and white Campions, Bluebells, spikes of Sorrel and many different grasses. As they lay there on the kitchen table in all their transient beauty I yearned to keep them as they were for always. The little house was full of jars and bowls and pots of this spring harvest for a week and then they began to die. As they died I watched them sadly and I wanted more than ever to keep them because they reminded me of my solitary but satisfying childhood in Cornwall. That was how the miraculous thing happened: because I wanted to keep those flowers – and others like them – for ever, I knew that I had to draw or paint them. I wanted to do it in the style of the old botanical illustrators, with all their precise exactness. It seemed practical to use those draughtsman's pens that never lack for ink, and that was how it started.

The first drawing was of some Arum lilies, surely an odd choice when my interest was mainly in wild flowers, but I have always liked the furling, curling coil of those creamy spathes. I drew carefully in pencil on the page and the miracle began to take shape – the lilies grew. I went to bed at dusk, exhausted, resolving to wake at dawn to continue. The next day I thought as I woke that it would all have been in my imagination and that when I went downstairs the paper would be blank. I was almost afraid to look, but there was the half-finished pencil drawing, and by evening it was done. The next two days were spent in carefully and rather laboriously inking over the work and finally it was complete.

Drawing became an obsession. I drew during the long, light summer evenings and got up early to draw again before my subject faded. I used every weekend to make more and different plant-studies because I felt that these drawings were to change my life: that first summer of discovery passed in a haze of effort. Then it was autumn, and it was time to do something about this new capability, now that I was sure that it was no temporary magic. The summer's drawings were awarded a bronze medal by the Royal Horticultural Society, and I met the dear and clever man who later became my second spouse. Suddenly and unexpectedly the thatched cottage came on to the market, and the owners wanted us to have it. There were very many difficulties but the call of the garden across the road was so strong that they seemed almost insignificant; also, my spouse-to-be was fascinated by the steep pitch of the thatched roof.

This seemed to clinch matters, and since that time I have spent all my waking hours gardening, drawing, designing, painting and writing, with the occasional stimulation of radio broadcasting to stir the adrenalin even more. The garden is the source and the cause of it all, and in the following pages I can share a year with you in my cottage garden.

Lys de Bray
Wimborne, Dorset, 1983

Arum Lily

1 January

Spring has come to the cottage garden very early this year, and many of the primrose-clumps beneath the apple tree on the bottom lawn are in flower in the thin, bright January sun. They are one tone with the pale sunlight, but the presence of their many wide-open flowers means that winter's memory is fast receding.

Under the un-named apple tree by the field gate there are the bright mischievous eyes of some crimson Polyanthus already in bloom, safely sheltered from any bad weather to come by all the taller plants around them and by the sheltering branches overhead.

Near the pergola which runs alongside the path leading from the gate to the front door of the cottage there is a small bed which curves suddenly out into the ever-decreasing area of the upper lawn. This bed has a group of Hellebores of several types, and though their situation does not strike me as being the best that I could offer them it is obviously very much to their liking because the clumps are increasing in size and floriferousness year by year. Under the weeping hair of the long Forsythia branches, inherited with the garden, there is a fine clump of Lenten Roses (*Helleborus orientalis*) also inherited with the garden, whose varietal name I shall probably never know. The lambent weather that we have been enjoying since November is very much to its taste, because there are more green-white flowers and buds than ever before.

Beside these is a comparable newcomer to the garden, *H. atrorubens*, planted three years ago, whose sinister wine-dark flowers show off their golden stamens most handsomely against the contrasting blotched and spotted crimson of the petals. Slightly to the right there is another expanding clump of *H. orientalis* with fine rose-coloured flowers, and this year there are nine flower-stems. Ever since I came to the garden I have been meaning to move the resident Hellebores a trifle further forward where they will not be so smothered by the summer growth that rises up in front of them.

Every year the Chaenomeles above them and the Forsythia behind them extend their branches a little further forward, making a dense canopy of leaves above their heads all summer long. Semi-shade is right for these south European plants, but in this garden they receive no summer sunlight at all and very little natural rainfall, and I am always surprised at their return to health and vigour in late winter and early spring. This year I really will move them all as soon as they have finished flowering, though *H. atrorubens* must wait until autumn – late October being the correct time to transplant this particular variety, whose leaves usually disappear completely in summer. The other two can be moved in March, which might possibly have been the reason for not having moved them in previous years; their flowers last in beauty for quite three months, sheltered as they are from the perversity of the elements. I seem to remember that I pruned the overhanging branches of the Chaenomeles and the Forsythia a year ago – straight into convenient vases, because the Hellebores showed no sign of fading.

9 January

The daisies are in flower on the lower lawn, as they have been for several weeks now. There is an old saying, 'When you can place your foot on seven Daisies, spring has come', but they are not quite thick enough yet. They probably know that the weather must inevitably take a turn for the worse, though there has been no rain for three weeks. This part of the lower lawn is very interesting in summer, because it was made of turf from a particular local field.

In high summer, when once or twice because of idleness or busyness I have neglected to mow the lawn, all manner of nice wild flowers colour the grass at the foot of the steps. There is Self-heal (*Prunella vulgaris*), Red and White Clover (*Trifolium pratense* and *T. repens*), Lady's Fingers (*Lotus corniculatus*), Ground Ivy (*Nepeta hederacea*) and what I always called 'Birdseye' as a child – the Germander Speedwell or *Veronica chamaedrys*, and, of course, the Dandelion and Daisies that are to be found in almost every lawn.

18 January

The Daffodil leaves are four inches high now and the *Helleborus foetidus* (which I refuse to call by its common name of 'Stinking Hellebore', preferring to speak of it as 'Bear's Foot') is in bloom with its singular flowers that are like loose green cups with purple or crimson edges, which look as though the flower has been singed. *H. foetidus* is a stiff and spiky-looking plant which has little natural movement. It has a sinister appearance, with leaves that resemble downward-pointing and grasping claws. This Hellebore's leaves are in two distinct tiers of colour, with the flower-scape topping all with its falling clusters of paler green bells. The lowest tier of leaves is the previous season's growth and is consequently a dull, dark olive-green, rusty and browned with age. The newer season's growth which began to form after last year's flowers had faded is a brighter and altogether cleaner green, and at this time of year the plant is very interesting with its three very clearly demarcated bands of colour. In my garden the plant flowers and then dies, which is not truly characteristic; in other situations more to its liking the plants will go on for several years, forming flower-buds in late autumn that will be in bloom just after Christmas.

The flowers do not wither in the normal way because the 'petals' are not petals at all, but developed sepals that remain as protection for the enlarging seed-vessels. This is why the 'flowers' of all this allied species, such as *H. orientalis* and *H. niger*, take many months to fade and disappear. The black seeds that eventually form are coated with a substance called an 'Elaiosome' that is attractive to ants, which in carrying the seeds away act as a living method of dispersal. *H. foetidus* prefers to grow in the light shade beneath deciduous trees in humus-rich soil which does not dry out. This is probably the reason why my own plants do not 'do' here, because the free-draining soil that is so good for many other species leaves the Hellebores and other woodland-loving species hanging suspended in light gravel. I am importing whole sackfuls of genuine leaf-mould for special plants, but this is a slow business.

The evening temperatures may become colder and colder until the thermometer begins to drop to several degrees below zero, where it will remain until long after dawn. I have often marvelled at the cellular strength of those apparently delicate petals which seem able to withstand these unkind extremes. There are two Vincas, *V. major* and *V. major aureo variegata*, which sprawl about in a very untidy way beneath the *Prunus pissardii*, looping and festooning the lower branches of the nearby *Cistus ladaniferus* and the Escallonia which grow there. I am very fond of Vinca, the Periwinkle, because it had such a useful career in the middle ages as a magical plant. No spell seemed to be complete without a portion of Periwinkle, whether for a flying-ointment, a love-potion or as a garland-flower for a cow's necklace which would protect it from the murrain.

Those were stirring and uncertain times, and I grow Periwinkle in memory of them. Their flowers begin to come in November after a late-autumn holiday, and though they are smaller than in summer, and sometimes on a particularly icy morning their petals are curled with the cold, they flower continuously thereafter for many months. I salute them because every week, no matter what the elements do to them, there are fresh amethystine flowers for the small vases in the house. It is worth taking a regular trot round the garden in the earliest days of spring to catch the first and unexpectedly forward flowers which might otherwise be missed.

Beside the Primroses the spears of the Spring Snowflakes (*Leucojum vernum*) are much taller now. Once a garden has known Snowflakes, Snowdrops somehow seem to be a lesser flower, though of course they are not. By comparison with the larger and more vigorous Snowflake (which entirely lives up to its name) Snowdrops (*Galanthus*) are smaller and shyer. Their leaves are a glaucous blue-green, which is quite a different colour from the altogether longer and larger

Periwinkle

dark green strap-shaped leaves of the Snowflakes. The six petals of the Snowflake are all the same size, whereas those of the Snowdrop are arranged as three small green-tipped inner petals enfolded by three long petals of pure white. The flowers are totally dissimilar, therefore, and are only compared with each other because they flower at the same time and in the same woodland conditions.

The Leucojum's nodding flower really does resemble a falling flake of snow because from a distance the pale green pedicel that supports it is almost invisible, and the flower seems to be momentarily caught in its fall to the ground. The bulbs are large and prefer to grow in slightly moist conditions, liking leaf-mould where possible and tolerating light summer shade. There is a taller cousin, the Summer Snowflake (*Leucojum aestivum*), which often begins to flower as *L. vernum* fades.

To follow on with the same family *L. autumnale* – the Autumn Snowflake (surely a contradiction in terms, even in our odd and irregular climate?) – flowers from July onwards, with the slightly pink-tinged flowers appearing before the leaves. This cousin needs full sun, coming as it does originally from Spain and North Africa. It is taller and more graceful than the other two, but of them all I like the Spring Snowflake best. The Snowdrops grow thickly beneath the huge Weigela by the pond, in drifts with the yellow Dutch Crocus and *Crocus tomasinianus*. The Snowflakes grow on their own, well away from the Snowdrops, under the apple tree on the lower lawn, though only as regards their species – they have gaily-coloured companions here which have been flowering in succession since October.

The apple tree is a giant among its kind, flowering and fruiting with amazing vigour in spite of its great age. It is an old-fashioned variety called 'Keswick Codlin', which is only seen nowadays in neglected orchards. The apples have the typical long 'Codlin' shape, and they are what I would have described in my schooldays of long ago as being 'scrumptious'. They begin by being tinglingly acidulous and full of juice, ideal for those first sharp-flavoured apple pies. Then there is a lull while they increase in size a little and gradually turn very slightly yellow-green. At this stage they are the most delicious eating apple that I have ever tasted, though they do not keep.

20 January

The Witch-Hazel (*Hamamelis mollis*) is in flower, and what a strange thing this is with its yellow spiders scrambling about all over the stems, but what fragrance these flowers have. This small tree – or tall shrub – will grow to a height of about ten feet (3m) in almost any sheltered position, though it is quite hardy. The flowers can appear very early in the year, from December onwards according to the general weather conditions, but the flowers can withstand zero temperatures and all the other seasonal inclemencies without harm. Wind will tear

Helleborus foetidus

the raggedy petals to pieces, which is why the tree is best planted in some sheltered corner. The summer leaves are rather average in appearance, closely resembling those of the Hazel (*Corylus* spp.), but they turn a fine, even butter-yellow in autumn. My small bush is in the middle of the herb bed where it will be able to extend its branches in comfort since I moved an over-large Fennel from its sunward side.

It has been so warm lately that I have daily expectations of seeing the Winter Aconites (*Eranthis hyemalis*) emerging backwards out of the ground as is their wont. These very early spring flowers are another member of the giant Ranunculaceae family, to which belong, though several times removed, such unlikely cousins as the Buttercup, Clematis, Peony, Monkshood, Hellebore, Delphinium, Rue, Nigella and Anemone. Aconites come up and out with such a rush that their first flowers can be easily missed. They break through the soil-surface with their flowering stems bent double – the cellular structure is thicker and stronger at this upper point than at any other – and the pale leaves trail last out of the ground, though these darken very quickly.

In a very short time, depending on the amount of sunshine that they receive, the stem straightens and elongates, and the fan of leaves flattens out to form an Elizabethan ruff beneath the golden chins of the glossy blossoms that look very like large Buttercups. These are lovely little flowers which appreciate the early spring sun. Inclement weather at their flowering time quickly fades the flowers and makes them transparent, and as they bloom so early they can often

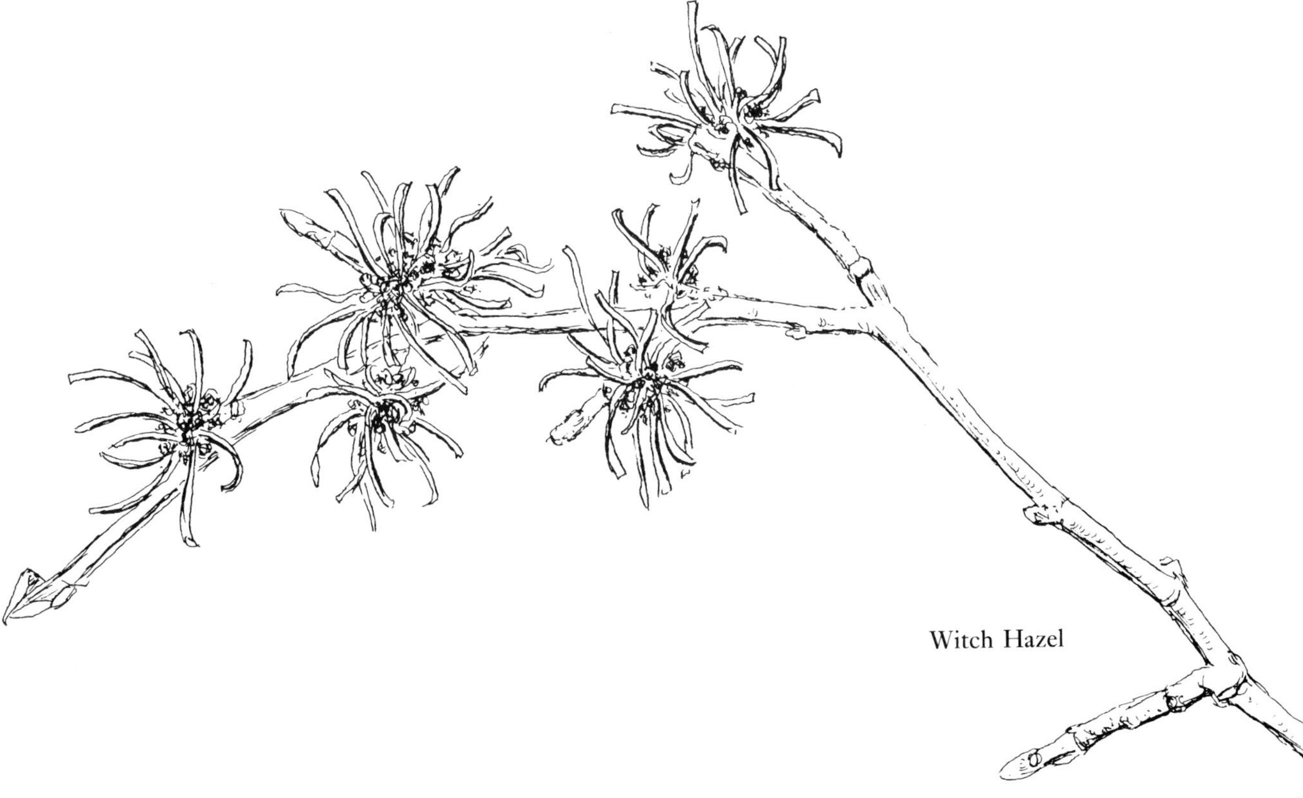

Witch Hazel

be seen emerging through a mantle of snow. The leaves of the Aconites disappear very quickly from the scene after the flowers wither, and the small wrinkled rhizomatous tuber will then become dormant for the remainder of the year. This is the time when these little plants are sold by garden centres because the tubers are easy to handle, but it is often very difficult to break their dormancy and there is much disappointment if the flowers do not appear the following spring.

25 January

Spring has now been properly heralded by the first Crocus opening its sun-coloured chalice on the lawn below the studio windows. Whatever the elements do between now and Easter the chorus of Crocuses will rightly tell me to ignore it. *C. tomasinianus* is usually the first to flower, but this year everything in the garden is coming along out of order. The exceptional mildness which is still continuing is not really a cause for rejoicing, because it is pulling the daffodils and other bulbs up by their boot-straps: I am quite sure that their growth is being too hastily forced. The warmth means that all the less pleasant inhabitants of the garden will not now meet their proper and rightful demise generally brought about by the usefully sharp frosts of early spring.

It is altogether very worrying because there has been hardly any cold weather since last November. I feel that the Sleeping Beauties of the garden, who need a period of proper dormancy normally engendered by a lengthy period of cold, will not have time now for their deep winter sleep. Under the propped Apple-tree the *Cyclamen coum* is still flowering – what a very un-English colour it is at this time of year, but how cheerful.

The sunlight shines on the convoluted branches of the Corkscrew Hazel (*Corylus avellana contorta*). This is a shrub that has nightmarishly curled and twisted branches which can only be seen properly when they are leafless – as now – or better still, when lit by the bright spring sunlight of today which makes the glossy light-brown branches come to life. In the summer the leaves follow the line of the branches, and because of the turns and twists of these the bush looks slightly seasick and I often have inquiries as to its health. The Corkscrew Hazel should be planted in a prominent 'winter' position where its strangeness can be appreciated for almost five months. The immutability of stone is the best possible background for the frozen movement of its polished branches, from which dangling catkins will later flirt with every passing breeze. However, it is less than exciting in summer, with its muddled foliage, so its siting should be very carefully planned.

My Corkscrew Hazel grows against an arm of the rock garden which extends across a path. Here there is a tumbled heap of Purbeck stone which was an afterthought to pond, water-garden and rockery, but which is very successful, incorporating as it does the oldest bird-bath in the world. This is a half-ton slab of the same Purbeck stone, with the imprint of a dinosaur's footprint in it which the birds use as a hip-bath in the evenings. The dinosaur that made the print walked across a bog a hundred and sixty-five million years ago (give or take a decade or two) and passed on into prehistory. This patch of mud would have hardened in the sun to become one with more of the same, lying undisturbed under further layers of forming rock for all those inconceivable millions of years. At a nearby quarry in the Purbeck hills (one of several) they specialize with practised skill in estimating where each of these footprints, which look like gigantic paw-marks, will occur next, and the quarrymen carefully chip them out by hand as curiosities.

Cyclamen coum

30 January

In the sunny corner near the field gate the first Celandine (*Ranunculus ficaria*) is in bloom beside the tree-stump. This tree-stump is semi-portable and has a large and comfortable hole halfway up it, in which I grew *Asparagus sprengeri* for the first season. This secretly spiteful fern, which has unexpectedly vicious prickles, looked very right with its arching sprays of light green trailing down from the hole, but I completely forgot about it until after the frosts came in late autumn, and so I lost it.

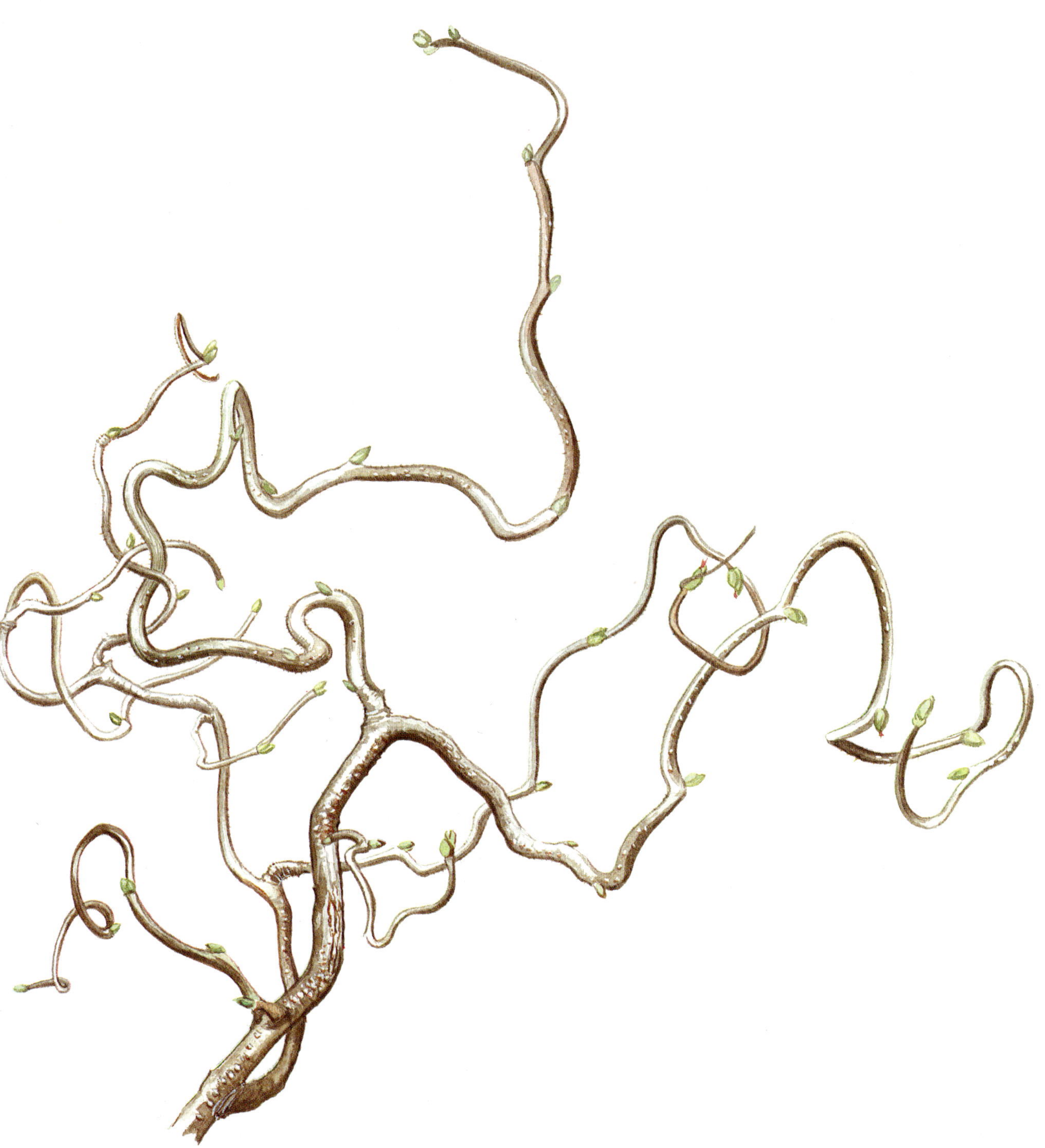

Corkscrew Hazel

The Daffodils under the studio windows are now seven or eight inches high, and the buds are clearly visible. This must be the most sheltered place in the garden, and I must remember it for future plantings. The white *Daphne mezereum alba* is out, with its waxen stars clustering along the bare twigs. *D. mezereum* is a very slow-growing bush, and as I survey this one, which is some 20 inches (50cm) high, I wish it were the commoner pink-flowered variety whose flowers retain their colour for so much longer. The flowers of *D. mezereum alba* turn brown when they have had enough and this looks unsightly (as does white Buddleia), whereas the now rare wild pink variety stays colourful for many weeks, fading slowly to mauve before the very poisonous seeds begin to form. The common name of this shrub is Mezereon, but most people call it Daphne.

The Cornus alba 'Elegantissima' under the sitting-room window is very handsome now with its brilliant winter-scarlet stems. These redder stems are the previous season's growth, the middle and oldest part of the bush having stems of a duller red. *C. alba* 'Elegantissima' is a good shrub for mid-winter, and it looks equally well planted by water, particularly when the snow is on the ground. The summer foliage is airy and delightful, being pale green edged with cream, and though the flat corymbs of creamy flowers are not particularly striking they are pleasant enough and somehow suit the shrub. Branches of the leaves are very beautiful indoors if they can be placed against a plain, dark background.

I was having to keep this lovely shrub pruned back unevenly at one time, because it was growing at the corner of the cottage and the branches were growing vigorously across the path. As it was a particularly rainy year I was getting tired of being sprinkled every day, so the vases were constantly full of the leaves, and the new growth from the base of the shrub was spectacular in the following spring. It throve on this treatment, growing ever larger and larger, so late last autumn I lifted several other less worthy things from the border under the sitting-room window and the Cornus can spread as much as it likes now in its new home. In the autumn the whole bush turns to an ususual shade of salmon-orange, which looks quite wonderful when seen through our iron-framed windows that are set with squares of blue and turquoise glass. If there is not the space in a garden for a large number of flowering shrubs – as here – then such space as is suitable should be given to those that have at least two seasons of beauty, if not three.

31 January

At last – the weather is seasonally cold and there is ice on the pond, though the morning is bright with sunshine and bird-song.

The *Garrya elliptica* looks like a decorated Christmas tree this year, with its 5 inch (13cm) long tassels that have the texture and shade of the most elegant pale green suede. This year the evergreen leaves of this slightly tender wall-shrub have not been scorched by the winter frosts because there have been none until last night. This is why the whole tree looks so handsome with its clusters of dangling, swinging 'catkins' that contrast so well with the rich dark green of the leathery evergreen leaves. *G. elliptica* will, in the fulness of time, grow quite large, so this should be considered when planting it, because it can reach a height and width of from 12 to 15 feet (3.4–4.5m). This shrub is dioecious, and if the interesting fruit is required, both sexes should be planted near each other.

In very mild districts *G. elliptica* can be planted in a sheltered garden in an open position and the swinging catkins are quite memorable when seen like this. It prefers a north-facing aspect, and for that reason is exceedingly useful on house walls, and will conceal an ugly building, or at least part of it. It dislikes being moved and will usually die if this is done.

The Hazel catkins are a-swing from the branches of the big bush in the field, and I make my yearly resolution to get to the nuts before the squirrels and mice.

I think that one of the most troublesome weeds of winter is the Winter Heliotrope (*Petasites fragrans*), even though the flowers smell most deliciously of almonds. This is a demon-weed whose roots will throw up enough leaves to smother the entire garden in a few seasons if it is not firmly checked. It was discovered in Italy in 1800 and was introduced to Parisians as a hardy winter-flowering plant. Sensibly, the French grew it in pots to perfume the winter air, and this is the only way to control it. If you have it in your garden, you will by now have discovered that it is almost ineradicable, and it is able to survive in the dry shade under trees and in any neglected and forgotten area. Shearing off the leaves regularly is one way of controlling it, because the rhizomatous roots can never be totally extracted from among tree-roots and from under paved paths.

Winter Heliotrope

2 February

It was not cold today and I went out for a much-needed walk to see what was doing in the hedgerows. Disturbed by my approach, the looping grey squirrels ran hastily across the road, and there was a sudden up-flying of rooks from the cornfield on the side of the hedge. They are already busy about their spring cleaning in the rookery that I can see from the garden seat.

In the garden the Wintersweet (*Chimonanthus fragrans*) is in bloom – what a strange blossom this is, not really attractive or even noticeable until one walks past the bush, and then ... that delicious scent. *C. fragrans*, otherwise known as *C. praecox*, is a rather inconspicuous deciduous flowering shrub that likes a south or west-facing wall for protection. The leaves are light green and pleasantly shiny, and it might be thought that precious wall-space is wasted on something which does nothing at all for its rent in the summer. In late December, however, or right up until February – as here – strange little pale yellow flowers suddenly appear on the leafless twigs, emitting a surprisingly heavy and spicy perfume which more than repays the minimal care and attention that this rather tender plant needs. The shrub will take several years to come to flowering and cannot be hurried. It will flower when it is ready, and not until.

Iris stylosa, or *I. unguicularis* as the Algerian Iris is now called, is in flower against the boundary wall. This is the winter-flowering Iris whose delicate blue flowers are so welcome at this time of garden paucity. *I. unguicularis* is another plant that needs to be placed in a position against a south-facing wall and then left alone. It needs no attention whatsoever, and though it is recommended in many of the gardening books that the leaves should be cut away a little in October merely for the sake of neatness, I do not do this because I have enough trouble persuading *I. unguicularis* to flower as it is, without annoying it in any way. It is the champion sulker of the garden, and if anyone moves it, as I did three years ago, it will cease most of its activities for this period, and even then may yield nothing in the way of blossom in the fourth year because of the excuse of a cold spring. But one sunny day in early spring the Iris flowers will suddenly be there; the buds look so much like the winter-browned leaves from which they spring that they are invisible from a few yards away.

6 February

The crocuses are coming out in a rush as they always seem to after the first few early flowers. This part of the lower lawn will be a pleasing sight in a few days, with all the separate patches of Crocus colours. Here there are 'Cream Beauty', whose name is an apt description for the flowers, and Crocus 'Blue Pearl', whose flowers have a pearly pale blue interior with a slightly darker tone on the outside that makes every single flower in a clump stand out as an individual. Crocus 'Zwanenburg Bronze' is a deep gold with stripes of mahogany brown on the outside, and as the flowers open in the sun they look very handsome. That old purple favourite, 'Remembrance', is always the last to flower here, and its larger buds are only just beginning to push their way through the grass.

Crocus Remembrance

Crocus aureus

8 February

The greenhouse is repaying all the care and attention that it has been receiving. The little orange tree in its pot has sweet-scented flowers and small green oranges, the Bougainvillea looks as though it may flower this year and the precious Orchid (this again was a gift) has produced four fine flower-spikes this season, which began, for the Orchid, in late October. It has green flowers with crimson splashes and is a variety of the large Cymbidium family. The plant surprised me by measuring nearly 4 feet (1.20m) across from side to side of the arching fall of leaves. It was a great pleasure to be in the same place with it for as long as it took to paint it, but, regretfully, it is now back in the humid warmth of the greenhouse which it prefers as any self-respecting Orchid would to the warm dry atmosphere of the studio. This Orchid may be stood outside in a sheltered position in good and settled summer weather, which will get rid of the whitefly that often affects the long-term residents of the greenhouse.

There is a tremendous interest in green flowers nowadays, and I seem to have quite a number in the garden, though I did not consciously go out seeking for them. For the collectors of green flowers there is a considerable list, among them being a rose, *Rosa viridiflora* or 'Monstrosa' (the green rose); green Gladioli; a delicious ball-shaped Chrysanthemum called 'Chartreuse' which is an even tone of acid green all over; an annual which is a little difficult to grow called *Molucella laevis* or 'Bells of Ireland'; a Tobacco-flower called 'Lime Green'; a Zinnia appropriately named 'Envy', some green-toned Tulips and Lilies and, of course, the several members of the Hellebore family that have green flowers – *H. foetidus*, *H. viridis* and *H. corsicus* (whose pale green flowers have now fully opened in the sheltered corner by the tree-stump). Opposite the studio door *Helleborus foetidus* is stiffly in flower with its three-toned tiers of green. Beside it is a tiny Daphne that I grew from a mere snippet which is only about 11 inches (27cm) high.

Orange

The wild Daffodils (*Narcissus pseudo-narcissus*) are in bud beneath the apple tree; there are a few clumps of these under the Weigela which I will move over after they have flowered so that all may be together. These little Daffodils are shorter than most of the cultivated varieties, with a delicacy and charm that their more vivid cousins lack. They have yellow trumpets and paler petals which grow unevenly and this gives movement to the flowers, whereas the petals of all the 'garden' Daffodils are placed evenly round the trumpet to produce a flat-facing flower.

19 February

Looking back, I realize that it has been a very busy year in the studio. One or two oddities had to be grown for the purposes of illustration, and these, I remember, I did find the time to cosset and protect from peril. One of these was the annual Holy Thistle (*Cnicus benedictus*), which was grown in medieval times for medicinal purposes. It is a very queer plant, with a rather meagre yellow flower that is protected by interesting crimson-black spines which seem to grow out of a silky fluff. It was very difficult to paint because the form of the flower-head was almost hidden by this same silk fluff.

Another oddity was *Citrullus colocynthus* or Coloquintida, which again was used medicinally in the middle ages. I managed to acquire some seed but I doubted my own abilities in getting it to germinate because it was three years old. Passing it on to my respected friend Tim, who has a gift for achieving horticultural miracles, I was rewarded in due course with the strangest of twining, scrambling plants, which had palmate greyish leaves and tendrils and small yellow

Wintersweet

flowers. It was most interesting botanically, but unlikely to win an award at Chelsea for anything whatsoever. Comparing it with some very accurate and academic reference late in the year at one of the university libraries, I was amused and a little annoyed to see that 'our' plants were not really the same as the reference which had been painted in 1930 and I can only suppose that the specimen plant had been slightly stylized, but I shall never know.

Cymbidium

Mahonia japonica

24 February

The crystalline fingers of frost are still floating on the pond and all the paths are cold to the soles of the feet. Since it was far too wintry to do anything useful outside, I retreated to the cosy warmth of the greenhouse, where soon I must make room for the seeds that I plan to sow. In previous years, in an excess of enthusiasm I have sown a matching quantity of seeds, and when they all germinated I had to find homes for them which in this garden in late May is next to impossible. Kind friends unenthusiastically accepted half a box of this and almost a full box of that, usually inquiring apprehensively 'How tall does it *grow*?'

It would seem that there is a definite place in the garden scheme of things for brightly coloured flowers that need no dead-heading, flower continuously from the end of May until late October, and grow no more than five inches in height. As far as I know, such a plant does not exist for our climatic conditions, and I wish that the plant-breeders would turn their attentions to producing one and would leave the old-fashioned flowers alone. So this year I will be sensible and will sow only half the contents of the packets or even less. Perennial plants are always worth growing from seed because they are so much cheaper, and it is possible to obtain unusual seeds sometimes, but not so easy to get the same species as a portable plant.

In the greenhouse the Arum Lily (*Zantedeschia aethiopica*) is sending up its fascinating, tightly furled spathes, already changing from green to cream. This plant always reminds me of the first flower drawing that I made less than ten years ago, and the subject then was an Arum Lily. Both the drawing and the plant have great sentimental meaning for me because producing that drawing changed my life completely.

All the Geraniums (Pelargoniums in actuality) are beginning to put forth smart new leaves and flower-buds. They recognize the approach of the 'long days' and many are in flower already. I am so fond of all of them, even the ordinary grenadier-scarlet 'Paul Crampel', that I would keep them all as they are by the end of the season if space permitted. As it is, I have to cut some of them short in order to be able to pack them all into the greenhouse for the winter, but I cannot resist popping some of the cuttings into a sandy compost, and of course, because it doesn't matter, they all grow like fun.

I know that to a purist Pelargonium-grower my plants are far too tall and leggy, but I place the shorter ones in front of them in descending height order and then there is a great bank of blossom in front of the cottage in July. I once saw a standard Geranium, grown like a Fuchsia, and this was about four feet high and was covered in flower. It was a truly lovely thing and was probably about ten years old, judging from the thickness of its stem. It is quite easy to grow them like this, but one must have a large greenhouse so that the potted plants can develop evenly all round the top.

Snowdrop

26 February

The icy wind that is howling round the studio is strong enough to move the stiff branches of the old apple tree. This is what I call real 'January' weather and it is very suitable for the time of year. The Snowdrops are out now, and their white flowers dangle in thick clusters beneath the leafless branches of the Weigela (*Diervilla florida*).

The peach tree that nestles against the sunny South wall of the house is just coming into flower, and its sugar-mouse pink flowers are reasonably protected by the overhang of the thatch.

The *Mahonia japonica* withstands the unkind wind very well, and its flowers, scented like Lily of the Valley, are just beginning to open, though they need the warmth of the sun to diffuse their perfume.

I think that the weed of the month is the Coltsfoot (*Tussilago farfara*), whose bright yellow suns have been open every fine day this month on the bank at the other side of the field where the soil is poor and dry. I am pleased that they are so far away from the garden proper, because this troublesome little plant is very difficult to eradicate once its rhizomatous roots have a grasp on your soil. Fortunately, it dislikes comfort and a soft bed – improve the soil and Coltsfoot will vanish. It was often called 'Son before Father' in former days because the flowers open on naked stems long before the hoof-shaped leaves. These are very attractive if one can dissociate one's aesthetic viewpoint from that of a gardener's practical one. Coltsfoot is still made into a herbal cough-remedy, and can be purchased in health-shops under the name of 'Coltsfoot Rock'. The plant was so much appreciated by the apothecaries of former times that a picture of the flower was used as the recognized sign for a herbalist's shop.

Coltsfoot

5 March

The sun is out and it is bright and warm again. I can see that the leaves of the Mandrake (*Mandragora officinarum*) are developing well. The Mandrake is sited at the sunniest edge of the herb-bed, because, after all, it was an important medicinal herb for our predecessors. However, I shall have to brave the legend and move it to a sunnier position – I'll borrow a black dog for the purpose, of course.

The rose-pink flowers of the Lenten Rose (*Helleborus orientalis*) are making a fine show under the black branches of the Chaenomeles, whose first few flowers are just beginning to open. The perfumed green bells of the Spurge Laurel are out. This little shrub is neither a spurge nor a laurel, its proper name being *Daphne laureola*, and as with all Daphnes its fruits are very poisonous indeed. Because the flowers are green and usually half-hidden by the downward-growing leaves they are often missed, but on a warm still spring day the strong Daphne-scent betrays their presence.

The Celandines are altogether too much of a good thing under the *Laburnum* x *vossii*, whose twisted trunk is of permanent interest throughout the year. The Lungwort (*Pulmonaria officinalis*) is out, with its blue and pink flowers rising from among the white-spotted leaves; the wild Daffodils are in delicate bloom a little further along by the trunk of the apple tree, and the Bluebell leaves are tall and vigorous everywhere.

12 March

In the night there was a heavy fall of rain which has beaten most of the Daffodils flat, so that their faces are lying in the mud of the flower-beds. When this happens, they seldom rise up again completely and the only thing to do is to go round and pick them, because the stems have usually snapped just at ground level. A gardenful of spreadeagled Daffodils is a sad sight, and when brought in for the vases they have to have their faces thoroughly washed.

The little early-flowering *Tulipa kaufmanniana* 'Shakespeare' has been quite unaffected by the elements, being only about six inches high. These are lovely flowers for so early in the year, opening almost flat in response to the rays of the spring sun, and in the autumn I shall obtain more bulbs of this and its companion in time the 'Water-Lily' tulip.

Later on the same day

The garden is losing its overall tone of winter brown – partly, I think, because the grass is suddenly a brighter green, but another reason is that the once entirely leafless shrubs are beginning to clothe themselves in all their many soft spring tones of leaf and bud. Many of these are very green indeed, but in others, such as the Snowy Mespilus (*Amelanchier canadensis*), the long leaf buds are a pale shrimpish pink. In the greenhouse the sweet-scented flowers of the small orange tree (*Citrus sinensis*) are out, filling the warm moist air with perfume. It really is a wonder that any of my Geranium-Pelargoniums survive this totally wrong environment, but survive they do.

Spurge Laurel

Lungwort

26 March

I have been away for two days, and on my return my first visit is usually to the greenhouse to make sure that the arrangements for its care in my absence have taken place. There my *Anemone coronaria* De Caen are all coming into bloom in their pots. These bright flowers will do perfectly well outside, though the flowers come a little later on in the year in time for late frosts that will destroy them utterly, which is why I keep a few in pots to brighten up both me and the greenhouse at this rather uncertain time of year. A succession of flowers can be planned by planting the corms at different times, though I think that this may only work well for the first year or so. After that the plants get sensible and flower when they feel like it, which is when the soil warms up properly.

As I walk down through the greening garden it is astonishing to see the rate of growth that has taken place in this short time. The Oxlips are all out now, and though some of the flower stems are short, they will grow longer as the days pass. I always hope that the bees will go back home and brush all the pollen out of their baskets after visiting my Primroses, because I simply do not want a group of False Oxlips, even though they are attractive. They have Primrose-sized flowers whose umbel has the growth-habit of the Polyanthus, that is, the short flower pedicels radiate from the top of the flower stem in a more or less even circle, whereas the flowers of the true Oxlips are smaller and paler, have a very sweet scent, and always hang over to one side. This is the way to recognize them, as they are exceedingly rare in the wild nowadays. The leaves of Oxlips (*P. elatior*) narrow abruptly to a stem, whereas the leaves of the other variety do not.

Anemone coronaria De Caen

Walking past the apple tree on the lawn, I came round the corner made by its trunk and stopped short with delight – the *Anemone blanda* have suddenly burst into flower overnight, it would seem, for their bright blue flowers are a complete surprise. *A. blanda* is a lovely thing for the early spring garden, being daisy-shaped and delightful, with flowers of an intense blue that makes a fine patch of different colour – different, that is, from all the many tones of yellow, pink and mauve. On a much closer examination, I find that the flowers of *A. blanda* are not truly blue, but are of an amethystine colour with darker bands, though on first sight they appear to be exactly the same colour as a Bluebell. Seen unexpectedly they have tremendous impact, and I hope that they will increase. There are other colours – pink, magenta, white and mauve – but none is as attractive as the blue, and fortunately one can always buy these corms separately.

Anemone blanda

28 March

A beautiful and sunshiny day, and I did justice to it by spending all of it in the garden. Walking quickly round before deciding where my proposed labours would have the best effect, there were many things to see. Most exciting were the fine flower buds and leaves of *Erythronium tuolumnense* 'Pagoda', and next to these another group of the tulip 'Shakespeare' were fully out, with their pointed pale yellow petals overpainted with scarlet. Nearly all the Daffodils are in bloom now, though in shadier places there are many more buds to open.

The Crown Imperials are out at last, though the slugs are doing terrible damage to some of the stems. What majestic plants they are, and how un-English and formal they seem in the March garden. The huge bulbs should be planted as soon as they arrive from the nursery, which is usually in early autumn (always buy from a reputable grower – imported bulbs may flower only once).

In the evening when walking back up the path to the potting shed with all the tools, I brushed against the Bay Tree (*Laurus nobilis*), which is inconveniently situated at the corner of the herb bed. Its flower buds are almost out, thanks to the mildness of the last few weeks, because this tree's buds are formed in the autumn and are carried through the winter, often and naturally succumbing to the inclemencies of our British weather. I say 'inconveniently' because it was very small when it was planted and now, as is the nature of things, it is not so small. One year it thoughtfully produced two seedlings, so I shall not disturb the surrounding ground now for several months, in the hope that this will happen again. The Weigela (*Diervilla florida*) is coming into leaf, and the big leaning apple tree that we love so much is covered all over with pale new silvery green leaves. The Kingcups at the edge of the pond are bright yellow and as cheerful as a smile.

Purple deadnettle

Crown imperial

Lesser Celandine

31 March

Wind and a little sun, and all the wild flowers are coming up everywhere. The Purple Dead-Nettles (*Lamium purpureum*) is very colourful in a sunny corner, and it is starred with late Coltsfoot flowers. I am rather glad that the Coltsfoot is flowering gaily on a gravelly hedge bank on the other side of the field, because it is an impossible plant to control in a (fairly) civilized garden. Above it Hazel catkins are swinging, and 'Pussy Willow' (*Salix caprea*) looks like silver rabbit's tails a little further on in the same hedge.

For my weed of the month I vituperately nominate the Lesser Celandine, pretty as it is in a woodland setting. It is entirely incongruous in my rose bed, among the tulips, choking the muscari, and tangling the forget-me-nots, and I *wish* it would go away. When I came to this garden there were only a few plants and these have spread and spread like the sands of the shore. The Celandine was formerly called 'Pilewort' because its fusiform tubers were seen to have an unfortunate resemblance to that particular affliction of civilized man. In an age of 'sympathetic medicine' the similarity between a plant and the disease that it was believed to cure was regarded as a clear indication of that plant's usefulness, and another example of this is seen in Lungwort (*Pulmonaria officinalis*), whose white-spotted leaves were supposed to resemble the diseased lungs from which the plant took its name.

Celandines regenerate from their tubers, which can easily break apart invisibly when the ground is weeded later in the year. The tubers grow from tiny bulbils that are found in the leaf-axils of unpollinated plants; these fall to the ground and are then washed away by the spring rains, to settle some distance away from the parent plant. Each tiny bulbil will grow into a tiresome tuber which will send up a healthy clump of leaves in the first year and a crop of smiling yellow flowers in the second, and the third, and the fourth, and so on. I have too many Celandines, and their dying leaves steal light and nourishment from worthier plants. The only way to get rid of them is to spring-clean – in mid-summer – the borders where they were thickest, and just beneath the surface of the soil will be found hanging clusters of the very recognizable tubers. Burn them or otherwise permanently destroy them – they are like Dragon's teeth in their regenerative abilities.

2 April

Every day in the garden things are bursting into flower now, and everything else is waking up. The first Bluebells are out, and I never cease to love them, particularly the white ones. In this garden they are more often than not very obliging because they seem quite happy to grow in uncharacteristically dry situations, providing a great deal of flower early in the year and tidily vanishing by midsummer. There was a fine old plant of the old-fashioned Candytuft (*Iberis sempervirens*) here when we came, and this 'easy' old thing now looks a little sorry for itself, with what appears to be frost-scorch on the leaves.

I have never known this very hardy plant to be tender before, particularly as it grows in a very sheltered position just under the three earthenware bread-crocks which are full of Narcissus and Wallflowers. I sheared all the damaged portions away, but, as is often the way at the end of a long day's gardening, I cut off a little too much and there among the sad pile of prunings were some unharmed shoots that were a fine dark green. I shortened them down and dipped the ends in rooting compound and put them all round the edge of an old clay pot in the hope that at least two or three will 'take'. I love the starch-white flowers of Candytuft – it always seems to me to be one of the whitest of all flowers and should have a home in every cottage garden.

The Kingcups (*Caltha palustris*) are at their best just now, with the young spears of *Iris pseudocorus* growing up all around them. The snowy plum blossom is springing into bloom on the dark-branched trees in the field. I wonder if the harvest from them will be as good this year – last season the branches were bent down under the weight of the ripening fruit. Plums seem to behave in an all-or-nothing way, so I think that I can forget about pies and puddings and jams this year. Certainly the bees from the hives in the field are doing their part already.

The flowers of the Snake's Head Fritillary are out at last – I have been waiting for these for some weeks, and have been inspecting them twice daily to make sure that no evil pest has found them. There is a strange colour among the white and maroon flowers, an odd sort of chequered, leaden shade that is impossible to describe. I am more delighted than I can say to see them, because I have tried many times to persuade them to grow and flower and hitherto have been unsuccessful. Now at last, here they are, a charming group of a dozen or so, all different heights and colours, some fully out and others with evil-looking downward pointing buds that have given rise to the very descriptive common name.

The Globe Artichoke (*Cynara scolymus*) which lives on the corner of the top lawn near the Amelanchia is putting out its toothed silver leaves. This is a large and handsome plant to grow in a herbaceous border, or where something sculpturally striking is needed. It needs plenty of roon in which to shrug its shoulders comfortably, and this I do not have, because its summer requirements are about six square feet of space. The huge leaves are always a pleasing shade of silver-green, with August-flowering 'thistles' in which the bees often go to sleep for the night. I always think of the flowers in August as 'Bee's Beds', having frequently come out during a warm evening after dark to count the number of sleepy bumbles who have decided that it was just too far to fly home that evening. I quite like Artichokes to eat, in spite of their being fussily messy, but would rather have the 'Bee's Beds' as giving more lasting pleasure all round, and in any case for four years running the Artichoke heads have suffered from blackfly, so there is an end to any prospect of eating them.

Yesterday, when I was down on my knees examining the soil of the wild flower border I was gratified to see that my Corncockle seeds (*Lychnis githago*) had germinated and are now at least 1½ inches (3cm) high. This now rare wild flower is very easy to grow and needs no cosseting whatsoever. The hard black seeds should be sown outside in the ground in autumn, with their position marked, and just left. I tried them in the propagator the first year that I was given the seeds, and absolutely nothing happened, a true case of killing with kindness. Recognizable weed seedlings should be carefully teased out of the ground, because they will have germinated earlier, as weeds always do in their effective struggle for survival. The seedlings have pointed grey-green leaves,

Wallflowers

and grow quickly once they are out of the ground, liking a sunny position best.

Corncockle was a detested weed of cornfields in medieval times, and its presence in the corn crop depreciated the corn's value because the black seeds specked the flour when it was ground. 'Clean seed' free of Bluebottles (Cornflowers – *Centaurea cyanus*), Corn Marigold (*Chrysanthemum segatum*) and our now not so familiar scarlet Field Poppy (*Papaver rhoeas*) were purged from the seed that was sown, and have gradually died out. Indeed, in the very earliest times the presence of Corn Marigold, or Gold as it was more often called then, was considered to be a crime and the farmer was heavily fined. I was delighted to see two cornfields near here bright with nodding Poppies last year and I went about smiling at the thought of them for the rest of the day.

6 April

The innocent-looking *Hemerocallis dumortierii* is growing well, its leaves are still upright because as yet they are only about 14 inches (35cm) tall. I have cleared plenty of space around it for its late summer foliage to flop into, and though this area looks very bare at the moment, I know that I will be feeling quite smug when this inevitably happens. The spring croo-crooing of the pigeons in the tall trees beyond the field is a soothing sound when one is on one's knees addressing the weeds.

In the greenhouse the pots of *Iris xiphioides* are doing well, with many buds along the leaves. This is that popular blue Iris that all florists have at this time of the year and I keep a few pots going in the greenhouse during the winter for the earliness of the flowers. After these are over I plunge them into the soil outside for the summer and let the leaves die down naturally, which they do because their job is done. After a brief rest I bring them into the greenhouse, long before the frosts, and start to water and feed them a little, and have often had flowers much earlier than this.

8 April

I awoke this morning to the pleasant sound of rain dripping off the thatch. By the time I was up the rain had ceased, and when I looked out all the newly forming leaves and buds of the rose 'Nevada' just outside the window were pearled and spangled with raindrops. Beyond them the new yellow leaves of *Physocarpus opulifolius luteus* by the stone seat are exactly the colour and shape of a Brimstone butterfly though they are as still in the early morning as a Brimstone butterfly never is.

The Daffodils would have been wonderful this year, especially 'White Lion', which is a handsome double variety with a white perianth and trumpet and an extra petticoat-frill of yellow petals among an inner row of white ones. In the mass these Daffodils look very well, especially against some sort of dark background, but this year the gastropods took a sudden fancy to them all, and climbed the stems each night to rasp away at the unfolding petals. It was truly heartbreaking, especially as most of them were new bulbs. But I still prefer the single Daffodil's purity of form – there is nothing to equal this.

The Pasque Flowers (*Anemone pulsatilla*) are coming out in the rockery. These have to be cosseted with chalky soil from a nearby quarry, but it is worth the annual effort. What delicate silky things they are – I grow only the mauve ones which are the colour of the now-rare wild flower. Pink, white, magenta and crimson kinds, though delightful and very beautiful, do not seem very characteristic to me. *A. pulsatilla* is called the Pasque Flower because it generally flowers at Easter-time. It has leaves, stems and the reverse of the petals all silkily furred with fine silvery hairs. Later the seed-heads are even more whiskery and last for many weeks. They are sometimes difficult to establish, but are worth any amount of trouble to get going. They would not do on clay soil, and are not happy in acid woodland conditions, and they need a well-drained position in full sun.

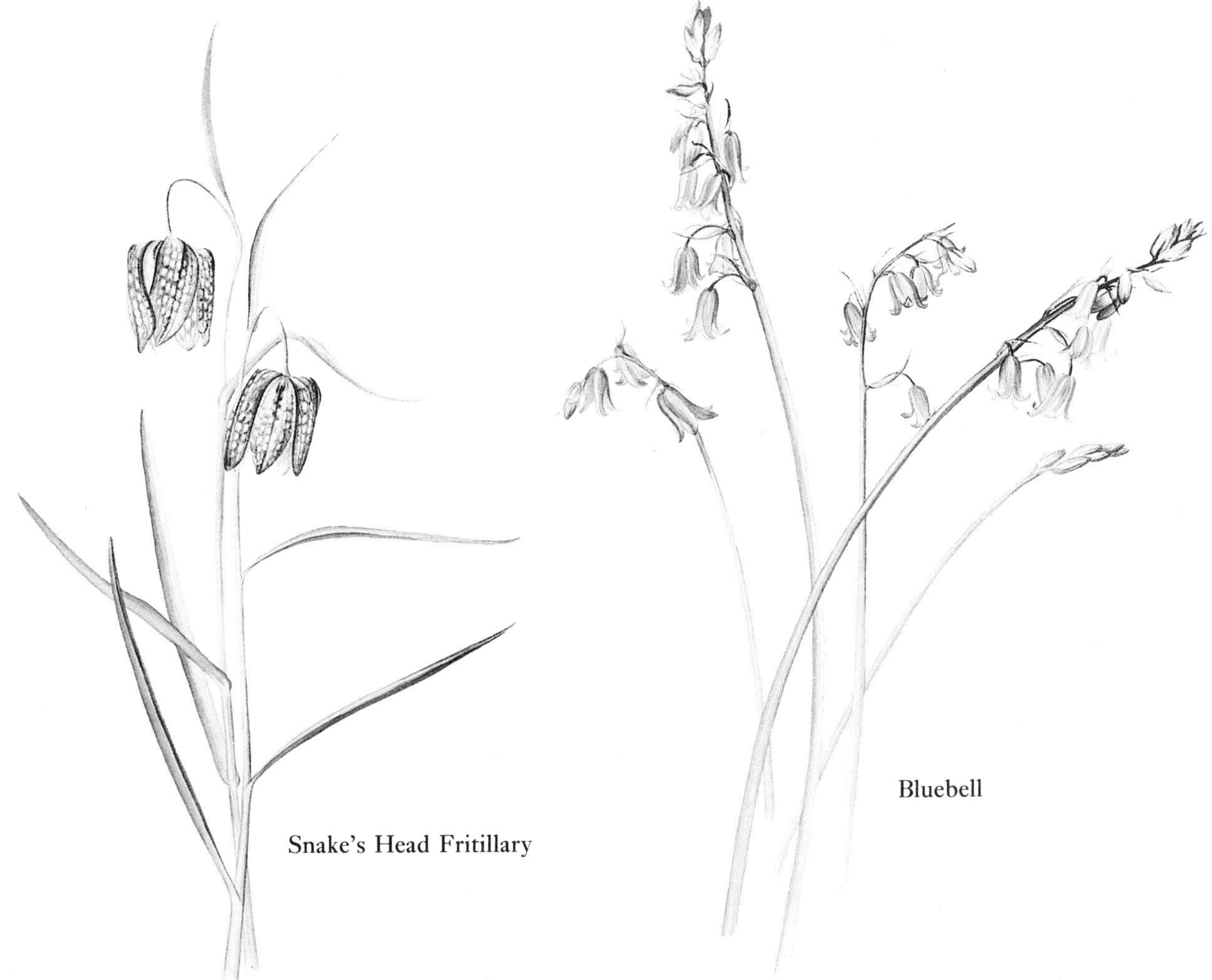

Snake's Head Fritillary

Bluebell

10 *April*

In the country hedges the Gorse is in full bloom, and there is white Sloe-blossom on black branches against the blue spring sky. The hedges are bright with the new green of Hawthorn leaves, which will hide the bird nests from view.

In the garden the *Erythronum* 'Pagoda' is fully out now, and its name becomes it very well – the turned-up corners of the petals are exactly like the turned-up corners of an old Chinese pagoda. My favourite Narcissus 'Actaea' is in bloom and is always the last to flower, except for the sweet-scented Jonquils. I wonder why the bulbs of 'Actaea' are so hard to find – it is a good old-fashioned variety that everyone can recognize, with a delicious scent that even attracts the early-flying butterflies.

Most of the seeds that I planted only a short while ago are up, but I am treating the seedling Morning Glories with extreme caution and respect – pride cometh before a fall, and anything could happen to them. For example, a particularly active and hungry gastropod might enter the greenhouse while the doors are open, slide up the staging to hide under it, and during the night that would be that! It has happened before, so now I have to scatter the floor with those unpleasant but so-effective pellets.

That old useful friend, the *Skimmia japonica*, is still in bloom, and on the female bushes can be seen fat scarlet berries which have been there since last autumn, beginning as green and changing gradually to cheerful scarlet. This happens only where there is a male Skimmia nearby. The male Skimmia bushes are usually shorter in height and have a domed inflorescence which is very distinctive. Both sexes are heavily scented, but when sniffed for the purpose and not accidentally in passing the perfume has an underlying unpleasantness. *Skimmia rubella* has pretty rose-coloured buds which form in the autumn and sit there among the neat evergreen leaves throughout the winter.

Pasque Flower

Cherry Laurel

Everywhere I go I see the flowers of *Prunus laurocerasus*, the Cherry Laurel, so beloved by the Victorians for its tolerance of almost any situation. It has perky tufting flower-spikes and this is the Laurel with black fruits. The other rather similar 'Laurel' is *Prunus lusitanica* which has later flowers that come in June and strings of scarlet fruits. This grows into a small tree, so beware of planting it as a hedge plant unless you really want 20-feet high privacy which this handsome shrub will ensure.

My friendly little yellow Corydalis (*Corydalis lutea*) is just coming into flower. This pleasant little plant inhabits all the spare cracks in the paving that the Alchemilla and the Fennel have not occupied first, and though it has rather soft and succulent leaves and takes some time to recover from being trodden on, it is so vigorous in its habit that it will always re-grow, particularly after a shower of rain.

All the Magnolias are out, balancing like shuttlecocks on their dark, invisible branches. I am thinking of the variety that is most often grown, *M.* × *soulangeana* which has full-bodied flower cups that sit on the branches and open upwards. This lovely thing comes in two colours – white with a feint dash of purple up the outside of the petals and a rich maroon colour which is *M.* × *soulangeana* 'Nigra', now more properly called *Magnolia lilliiflora* 'Nigra'. There are very many other varieties which are not so often grown as they could be, perhaps because they need a little more care and usually) a very sheltered position. *M. stellata* is exquisite, as its name implies: when it flowers it is like a cloud of fixed white stars, and these are deliciously scented. The form of the flowers is not so perfect as the chalices of *M. soulangeana*, but it more than makes up for this with their profusion and perfume. Another very interesting Magnolia is *M. sieboldii*, with pendant white lily-shaped flowers which obligingly hang downwards from the branch: in youth the flowers are difficult to admire, unless one prostrates oneself on the (usually) muddy turf of an April lawn, but as the shrub grows slowly to its full height of about 15 feet (4.5m) one can gradually assume a crouching position, and in the fulness of time stand erect to gaze up at these very beautiful flowers, silhouetted upside-down against the sky.

14 April

I try to keep the whole of one side of the garden for some of our dwindling collection of wild flowers. I have grown most of them from seed, and of course they are spreading about all over the place, particularly the Corncockles, which have taken to the garden in a very satisfactory way. So much so that this year they need thinning out. The Cowslips never seem to mind being moved, even when in full flower (as now) and do not even wilt. I have a friend who has a strange shady pond in her garden, and a clump of Cowslips appeared at the edge of it one year. They grew and grew and waxed simply enormous, producing flower-stems that were 9 to 12 inches (23–30cm), which I have never seen before. The plant was large in all its parts, proving that a change of habitat will change the plant's appearance greatly.

The *Akebia quinata* creeper that almost covers the remainder of the shed is now in full glory of blossom. The individual three-petalled flowers are not instantly striking, but when the whole thing is seen as a scented crimson curtain that drips down the wall it is very rewarding. This is certainly its best year to date, almost probably attributable to the mild winter, though in part it may be due to the fact that the Akebia has been here for five years now and is truly settled.

The garden has become a tonal symphony of green, with bright notes of blossom appearing everywhere. The Clematis 'Blue Lagoon' is in flower, and I reaffirm my vow to move it to a kinder place. Nodding Narcissi, bright stately tulips, dangling crimson tassels of American Currant, sweetly scented Wall-flowers (to counteract the tom-cat smell of the American Currant) and Bluebells of every possible shade are everywhere. The double-flowered Kerria, the ornamental Crab-apple 'Profusion' and the heady scent of the sweet violets that grow opposite the studio door. The purple ones – *Viola odorata* – are more instantly visible, but the scent of the white flowers seems to linger just that little bit longer. The perfume of Violets numbs the olfactory nerves, so that the scent seems to disappear while one still has one's face buried in a large bunch of these romantic flowers. But the scent has not gone, of course, and if you leave the flowers for a while and then come back to them you will be able to smell them just as before, and, just as before, the scent will appear to die away.

15 April

A warm and sunny day, and basking on the leaves of the Hypericum 'Hidcote' was a queen wasp, obviously very exhausted from her food-gathering. Queen wasps in April are almost as harmless as kittens, unless deliberately annoyed – they are too tired and too busy to bother about anything but the survival of their species. Wasps are excellent creatures to have in our gardens, doing more good than the harm that is often attributed to them, and this is why they are no trouble to us early in the year.

Everywhere now the blossoming trees are a cloudy mass of flowers – so many shades of pale pink, some deeper and some brighter, and some exactly the same colour as sugar mice. There are many shades of white too, though this may sound rather strange.

This was a very good day for being out in the garden, and I was able to welcome the returning house-martins as they flew overhead; the swifts come later on.

Clematis macropetala 'Blue Lagoon'

Honesty

25 April

Last night, snow fell. The soft, wet flakes did not lie, though the temperature dropped considerably and I went down to make sure that the greenhouse heater was functioning properly. In the morning, when I went out to see how the garden had fared, there was a light fall of petals beneath the apple tree: there will not be so many apples this year perhaps, but I shall not mind because the plenitude that we so undeservedly enjoy is an embarrassment in the autumn.

The Laburnum is just coming into flower. This particular tree has a very attractive shape with a trunk that forks some two feet from the ground with the two stems continuing to grow closely and gracefully together. I always think of two Victorian sisters every time I look at it and, casting my mind back to my childhood, I seem to remember visiting a house that had statues everywhere. Among them was a life-size marble of two gracefully posturing maidens, and the tree reminds me of these.

Honesty is in vibrant colour in all the darkish corners where I have cunningly transplanted its temperamental seedlings. These hate to be disturbed because they have a long tap-root like a carrot, and can only be moved when very young. Honesty is a very amiable plant that will grow quite well in shady places which it will light up with a flourish of magenta, loud as a bugle at dawn.

I nominate as weed of the month the Dandelion (*Taraxacum officinale*). I do not mind Dandelions on road verges in spring, where they make a ribbon of golden yellow that echoes the curve of the road, and I think that a Dandelion clock is one of nature's most beautiful pieces of architecture. But what I do mind is the product of that clock, the several hundred or so parachuting seeds that all seemed to float to rest on my small lawns when I had thought that *all* their cousins had been consigned to the bonfire. I spent many backaching hours clearing the lawns of Dandelions because their flat 'plates' of leaves were preventing the grass from growing and were themselves growing ever larger. Unscathed by the lowest of mower-settings, the flowers were forming as flat as an opera-hat to smile upwards infuriatingly. (All gardeners will know about the smile of a victorious Dandelion.) There are many useful purposes for this plant as a salad vegetable, as a mild diuretic and as a rather tame coffee, but I shall begin once more on the lawns while the new plants are yet young.

7 May

It has been raining for about a fortnight, and the garden is very green indeed. Almost everything is in full leaf now except for such late-comers as the Ginko, the Robinia and the Fuchsias. All this rain has made the lawn as green as grass should be, though it is overdue for a haircut. It looks like a spring meadow with Daisies, Plantains and the doomed Dandelions, with here and there the lavender-coloured flowers of Ground Ivy and some courageous Buttercups. As may be gathered, the rain has given the Dandelions a reprieve, but this is only temporary.

Under the apple tree the delicate froth of Queen Anne's Lace (*Anthriscus silvestris*), perhaps more commonly but less attractively called 'Cow Parsley', has become quite tall. *Rosa longicuspis* has grown up through all this prettiness with shining new leaves, though as yet there is no sign of any flower buds. There is plenty of time for these to form because the rose does not flower until June. These strong tree-climbing roses often take two years or so to settle down, but after that they are gloriously abundant in their blossoming. I saw my first Orange-tip butterfly alight on a Periwinkle flower – both complemented each other beautifully in their colouration.

The leaves of the huge clump of Irises in the pergola bed have been growing apace recently – they like this weather at growing time, and today I noticed the dark colour of pointed flower-buds among the light green of the leaves. In the same bed the Lilies of the Valley are out, and each year they are more successful in their attempt to colonize this flower-bed. However, because they are such a charming and appropriate flower to greet visitors to the garden, I must allow them another foot or so of territory. The bright scarlet berries that often appear later on in the year are very poisonous indeed, but they can be dried and sown to produce new plants if the existing patch is not spreading quickly enough.

13 May

The shrieking magenta flowers of the Honesty are just going over now. I truly love Honesty because it has such an excellent survival rate, but this year the finest clump of all is most generally viewed against the distant lemon-yellow of the emerging Laburnum flowers, and a more terrible colour contrast cannot be imagined. The Grannybonnets (*Aquilegia vulgaris*) are out all over the place as they always are, and they are truly welcome because of their vigour and vitality and there are so many that the flowers can be spared for the first tall vases. A mature plant is a very imposing sight, often three feet in height with many flowering stems whose colour varies from palest pink (lovely with the first ferns) through mauve, pink, deep pink, purple and deep violet. They are very common cottage-garden flowers, often scorned by the more sophisticated, but I would rather have the back of a border quite full of these in all their colours than empty spaces. The leaves are very attractive and are evergreen here, providing patches of jade green ruffles throughout the winter.

Ground Ivy

Sweet Woodruff is out beneath the apple tree, starry with its tiny bright white flowers. This is an Elizabethan strewing herb whose flowers and leaves have no scent when alive. It is when the leaves are gathered and allowed to dry naturally that the sweet scent of new mown hay appears, and Sweet Woodruff is still used today as part of the filling for herb pillows. The scent lasts for years and the dried leaves placed beneath the lining paper of shelves and drawers will perfume their contents for many a season.

The plant that I value most in the garden is out at last – *Paeonia mascula*, the Steep Holm Peony. This is one of the most beautiful of our 'wild' flowers (it was introduced to this country in the thirteenth century by monks who came to found a small monastery on the Island of Steep Holm in the Bristol Channel). My plant has been grown from precious seed, and this is only the second time that it has flowered. Its huge, brilliant pink single flowers are the largest wild flowers that we have, and are certainly the most striking.

The sun is just coming out, and one of the nicest things about working in the studio is that all round me is the greenness of the garden. When the windows are open, as now, I can hear a blackbird singing his heart out in the apple tree that overhangs the field gate. There is nothing that tranquillizes the spirit more gently than the song of a blackbird in an English garden in spring.

Steep Holm Peony

The evening of 18 May, 10.30 pm

There were two small happenings today which brightened a time clouded by many problems. In the morning, as I hurried through the heavy rain to the studio, my eye was caught by the unexpected sight of a small lily in flower beneath the *Akebia quinata*. Heedless of the downpour, I knelt down in amazement, the better to examine it – I had never seen it before, nor any Lily like it. How did it come here? It must have come into the garden as a seed from one of the nurseries, but which nursery, and what lily is it? Mysteries like this are delightful and one can leave part of one's mind puzzling over them for days.

The other pleasant happening came as I was sleepily walking up to the house late in the evening after a very long day's work at the drawing board. As usual, I was accompanied by all the cats who were not particularly hungry, just glad to see me again. In the windy dark, with the rain still falling heavily, I heard a vigorous 'huffing' sound, quite close. I stood quite still to locate the noise, and the huffing came again, from the clump of Bamboos at the side of the studio. It sounded like the noise made by a Hedgehog, newly woken from his hibernation and going briskly about his nocturnal business. Hedgehogs are comparatively unafraid of humanity, so I went over to the corner and shone my torch among the dripping vegetation and the dead and curling leaves of the Bamboo that covers the ground here. And there he was, a small fellow about 8 inches long, very healthy looking, with a round bright eye which was regarding me with impatience as if to say 'Well, here I am, and now you've seen me, you can turn that thing off. I'm hungry, and you're frightening all the beetles away, stamping about like that.' I bade him 'good hunting' and went up to the cottage through the rainy darkness, happy in the thought that he had the whole night before him in which to stuff his small stomach with my succulent slugs. I am delighted that he is back again, and hope that he will bring all his relatives.

The Monkshood is in sinister flower. This is surely, apart from Laburnum, the most deadly thing that we can grow in our gardens. Monkshood (*Aconitum napellus*) is sometimes called Aconite, though it is not to be confused with the Winter Aconite, which though of the same family, *Ranunculaceae*, is a cousin several times removed. The other old name for Monkshood was Wolf's Bane, because the poison from the plant was extracted in order to tip arrows and spears so as to be sure to kill the marauding wolves of medieval times. In those times, every man grew his own poison, more to dispose of vermin than his neighbour, though in former days life was cheaper.

The whole plant of *Aconitum napellus* is poisonous, though the root contains most of the deadly aconitine that is capable of killing within 15 minutes of ingestion. The plant has always been used medicinally, and is still used today as a painkiller, a sedative and a febrifuge. Minute amounts of it are used in preparations that ease the pain of arthritis, sciatica, gout, neuralgia, rheumatism and specific chronic skin problems. This is no plant to experiment with, however, as it is quicker in its action than prussic acid and just as permanent. Monkshood is said to prefer a semi-shady position, but in this garden it does exceedingly well in full sun, but perhaps this is because it likes the garden. The plant was here when I came and I often wonder how old the various clumps are. It is increasing vigorously every year, and the earliness of its light green leaves is so welcome that I leave it be.

20 May

Finishing work very late this evening, I was coming back up to the cottage by torchlight. Near the bootscraper I saw a familiar hummock on the path, with all the cats grouped in a friendly and interested manner around it. It was the hedgehog again, nearer the house than I have ever seen him. I think that he and the cats have probably met on many occasions, because they were not particularly interested in each other. As I stood quietly watching, the hedgehog suddenly rose up from his crouching position and ran off on his tiny, neat feet. The cats took no notice of his departure and wandered off independently to look for something less effectively gift-wrapped.

22 May

The day started very dull with a forecast of rain to come, and as if to laugh at this, the sun shone gaily all the afternoon. The *Viburnum tomentosum mariesii* is out beside the stone seat – what a beautiful shrub this is. It grows relatively quickly in horizontal layers, with rows and rows of marching white flowers that perch in crowds all along the branches.

Lily of the Valley

23 May

The swifts are back, wheeling and swooping and screaming in the clear spring sky. What an eerie harshness it is, up there in the middle air. I notice that they begin their cries at about 5 o'clock in the afternoon, regardless of the weather. Presumably the insects that constitute their diet have risen in the warmer thermals that come up from the land in the late afternoon. Swifts spend their entire lives in the sky, having adapted through the ages to sleep, eat and mate on the wing, only returning to man's habitations to construct a simple and rather primitive nest in which to lay their eggs. The parent swifts have ceased to use their legs as other birds do, and if by some mischance they are forced to land on the ground they are unable to take off again without assistance. I remember once finding a swift on the muddy shores of a stream and I was able to pick it up and toss it into the air.

Monkshood

29 May

That other handsome shrub, *Cornus kousa*, is out, with its pointed four-petalled 'flowers' that will stay unfaded on the branches for months. The old Peonies are in blowsy bloom, and though this variety is seen very often, it is a satisfying colour to have in the spring. There are many more flowers than usual at this time of year, though all are bowed down with wet from the constant rain that is too appropriate for the month of April.

The Pansies are coming out in their many colours. When gazing down at an edging of them, I always think that they have such honest faces. However, if one looks, here and there one can find, all too easily, a dicontented-looking flower, or a sad one, or a simple one, or even an angry one. Sow a packet of mixed pansy seeds and see.

The Lilac (*Syringa*) is out, and I wistfully wish that all the best flowers were not twelve feet up. Over the years I have picked from the reachable areas of the shrubs, and as Lilac does not like anything at all being done to it, it takes two or three years to flower again lower down.

Across the field the Hawthorn hedge is in bloom, a creamy mass of flower that must never be picked for the house. I always feel that a hedge consists of Hawthorn, whereas the solitary trees that stand so mysteriously alone are May-trees. The worst of all bad luck came to anyone who brought branches of May-blossom into the house: death or sickness would surely result, a murrain fall upon the cattle and at the very least the milk would go sour and the butter would not come.

31 May

It is the last day of May, and all the wild flowers of the meadows are flowering as never before because of the mild winter and the warm damp days. Lady's Smocks flutter among the new grass with the Buttercups and the Ox-eye Daisies, and Early Purple Orchids grow in moist secret places.

Tomorrow it will be June.

In this garden the weed of the month is the White Deadnettle (*Lamium album*) which, to its credit, is quite harmless. It is a rather sly thing here, creeping about at the back of the border and underneath other things in a quiet and insignificant way until, hey presto! – there are the flowers, and one is condemned for neglecting the weeding. I like to see this plant growing on a country verge, or in a damp ditch or even in a hedge, and in all these places it looks very interesting. This is where it belongs. It does not suit a neat border.

Lilac
White Deadnettle

2 *June*

June – a month of rapturous roses. Yesterday I picked my first true bowlful of them; hitherto the bushes have been able to spare only one or two every other day except for 'Nevada'. To go with the roses and the month, the first of the strawberries are ripe.

8 *June*

As I went down to the studio this morning through the wet garden I saw a foolhardy frog being pursued in its zig-zag progression by an excited cat, who was following it in exactly matching zig-zag leaps. The frog hopped one last mighty hop into the safety of the pond, followed right to the edge by a very puzzled cat who stood with the turgid green ripples from the splash actually lapping over her furry toes. She peered anxiously into the duckweedy depths and was obviously thinking 'What strange mice there are this year!'

There has been much rain during the last few days, and the bronze Fennel that grows from a crack in the paving just outside the front door is misted all over with the most delicate sheen of tiny droplets that look like a scattering of diamond dust in the bright sunlight.

All the herbaceous Geraniums, which are the true Geraniums of course, are in flower. They form great hummocks of colour and particularly fine this year are the vigorous 'Johnson's Blue', 'Mrs Kendall Clarke' and *G. ibericum*, each of which is some 4 feet (122cm) across. These Geraniums are deceptively decorous when purchased but should nevertheless be planted some way back from the edge of the border, lawn or drive, so that they have plenty of room to flop forwards, which they most certainly will within three years. In winter it is very easy to forget the diameter of the clump and plant something else in the apparently empty space surrounding it, but this new treasure will be engulfed in May and drowned for ever.

For a very lovely association of plants, tall blue *Iris Chrysographes* or *I. Sibirica* can be planted at a safe distance just behind the Geraniums, and shades of blue Delphiniums behind these. All the flowers bloom together, and there is a beautiful range of blues and violets to choose from, with the extra interest of the pale green sword leaves of the Irises as a sharp break between the hummocks of the Geraniums and the rather bare stems of the Delphiniums.

Rose Zambra

Iris sibrica

The first of the herb-flowers are coming out, and among these I always include the Marigold (*Calendula officinalis*), whose petals can be used as a good colouring for rice instead of the expensive and now difficult to get Saffron (*Crocus sativus*). Rosemary is a strange shrub that can be uncharacteristically in bloom at Christmas shivering bravely in the winter wind; or, more sensibly and safely, it will begin to flower in May if the weather is warm. Thyme (*Thymus vulgaris*) is just coming out here at the edge of the path by the rockery, and the stately Angelica is very early in flower this year. The botanical name for this plant is *Angelica archangelica* which, for once, is harmonious and beautiful. Angelica is a tall biennial that produces large spherical heads of greenish yellow flowers, that are not in themselves attractive, but are handsomely sculptural when seen as a part of the plant when it is in flower.

Bees and flies are always busy around the large Angelica flower-heads, but never butterflies, because the flower is not the right shape for their long tongues. The seeds should be sown next month, or at the latest in September, because they do not remain viable if kept until spring. The little seedlings will pop up very quickly, and will be able to do sufficient growing to keep them going during the winter, though if a group of these large and handsome plants is really needed the seedlings should be given some sort of protection from winter frosts. The best way is to sow them in pots and winter them in a cold frame to plant out in the spring. They will not flower that year, but will shoot up like beanstalks in the late spring of the third season to flower in early summer. They die after flowering unless there is an offshoot growing on from the roots, though this does not often happen.

15 June

Each day in the garden some new beauty shakes out the creases in her petals. Today it is the turn of the Poppies, and the scarlet taffeta of these oriental beauties is brightly blazing in the hot midday sun. But over the fence and across the field there are the country cousins, whose gipsy skirts are almost exactly the same shade of scarlet, though the flowers are much, much smaller.

Every day as I go down to the studio I subconsciously notice the various levels of bird noise in the garden. I say 'subconsciously' because I am usually thinking about the day's work and how to get more of it into that same day than is often humanly or socially possible, and I say bird 'noises' because very frequently the noises that the birds make in and around the garden cannot be classed as song. Angry blackbirds sit on safe twig-ends of apple trees, squawking noisily at somnolent cats asleep on the warm flat stones of the rockery. Naturally the cat is as aware of the bird as the bird is of the cat, but the dignities of both must be observed, and therefore that cat is pretending to be asleep, though no animal could ignore the loud and repetitive noise less than fifteen feet away.

Another bird that makes an astonishing amount of noise for its diminutive size is a cross wren. This tiny bird will perch on a bramble and chatter and racket away like a demented clockwork toy. It is amazing to locate the source of all this noise and to find that it emanates from Britain's smallest avian throat. It must certainly be that there is a nest very near, because last year I heard this noise for the first time from the same patch of brambles, and this year it has been a daily occurrence.

Marigold

Delphinium

21 June

All the Clematis are doing well this year, and I surely do not deserve the fine show of bloom that they promise, judging by the number of buds still to open. Clematis have one rather tiresome trait, apart from their tendency towards wilt, and this is their habit of flowering at the top of wherever they have grown to, be it archway, pole or pergola. The flowers of most of them can best be enjoyed from an upstairs window, but it is not always convenient to ask one's visitors to lean out of the bathroom casement in order to admire the absolute perfection of the huge lavender-blue flowers of 'Lasurstern' or the brilliant crimson ones of 'Ville de Lyon'. Our cottage is a single-storey thatched building and we have no upstairs at all, so my Clematis can only be admired from the top of a step-ladder. These are hybrid varieties and should have been trained correctly in their younger days to prevent some of this 'top-flowering', but I encouraged their growth with manure-water (they are gross feeders) so effectively they were up and away in no time.

Another reason for hastening the formation of their woody stems was so that the gastropods should not ravage them. The flowers are produced on short lateral stems from the previous season's growth and some bloom has to be sacrificed initially to get a well-formed plant. One has to be cruel to be kind with Clematis, and after their first year in your garden they should be cut back in their second spring to within 12 inches (31cm) of the ground. When attempting to tidy up a well-grown Clematis in late summer, it will be found that the leaf petioles, which act as the plant's climbing aids, are so intertwined one with another that it is not possible to untangle them. They do not take kindly to being untwisted from each other and will break, but this does not matter as they will soon grow new leaves and stems.

24 June

Nearly all the roses, if not out, are at least showing colour in their buds. An English garden in June is not truly representative of England unless it has roses, though I think that this particular garden has become a little more representative than could be expected for its size. The rose bed outside one of the bedroom windows is bright with colour, though it is not quite as harmonious as I would wish, owing to inadvisable haste in the spring planting. It was a *very* cold day.

The modern hybrid tea 'Harry Wheatcroft' is out and its astonishing flowers, uniquely striped and splashed red on yellow, associate well with its neighbour 'Joseph's Coat' which is a brilliantly coloured orange/yellow floribunda with climbing tendencies. However, they clash quite horribly with the ice-cream stripes of the Gallica 'Rosa Mundi', whose bush is already covered with its beautiful flowers. Rosa Mundi's blooms change in tonal quality: initially they have bright cerise stripes, splashes and spots on the palest of pink backgrounds, but as the days go past these markings age gracefully to a pleasing magenta-mauve with what seems to be the overspill of background colour changing delicately to match; as one gazes at such a bush it is a marvel to see that each one of perhaps fifty flowers is completely and absolutely different from its neighbour. 'Rosa Mundi' is an excellent wet-weather rose, and as I woke to much-needed rain this morning I knew that all the open flowers would be undamaged, unlike many another more modern beauty. Notwithstanding the charm of the striped flowers with their bright gold stamens, this rose is sturdy enough to be used as an internal garden hedge.

Clematis 'Ville de Lyon'

My beloved Sweetbriar (*Rosa rubiginosa*) is out now, its small pink flowers bright against the light green leaves that are giving off their delicious apple fragrance in the warm, moisture-laden air. This is another sturdy rose that can be used as a hedge, to be strategically sited so that the prevailing breeze can send scented zephyrs throughout the garden during the summer. Sweetbriar is a very strong-growing rose, not attaining more than a maximum 5 feet (152.05cm), but it should be pruned back immediately after flowering to encourage late summer growth, because left to itself it will grow tall and leggy. It produces handsome urn-shaped hips for early autumn and these can be left on until winter, but a second tidy-up at this time will promote growth where it is needed – at the base of the bush.

The sun-yellow flowers of the *Hypericum patulum* 'Hidcote' that overhang the boundary wall are just beginning to come out, and this is now a truly enormous shrub. The variety most usually seen is *H. calcinum* or 'Rose of Sharon' which is used by municipal authorities in desperation as a no-trouble, no-effort, no-maintenance form of ground cover, where it acts as a trap for paper, cans, bottles and all the other detritus of urban humanity. However, this plant is so willing to grow almost anywhere and even to flower in shady places and under trees, that it is frequently put upon and then scorned for its good nature. It spreads stoloniferously for an indefinite distance and the tough stems act as an all too effective trap for rubbish. *H. patulum* 'Hidcote' is an easy shrub which thrives in full sun, though it will perform reasonably in shadier situations. It will be a huge splash of jolly colour for over a month now, with a later and lesser flowering at the end of August and the beginning of September.

Common Thyme

The studio in summer

The bright flowers of the old-fashioned Rose Campion (*Lychnis coronaria*) are just beginning to open near the junction of the paths at the corner of the cottage. This is a plant whose brilliant magenta flowers are softened by the silky grey leaves and stems and it seeds freely, though a wet spring will carry off the tiny silvery rosettes that are so charming. Seed should be collected from the rattling seed-heads in August or September and dried, and this can either be sown immediately and overwintered in a cold frame, or sown in spring to grow on in the usual way. Rose Campion thrives in poor soil, but it must have full sun. The leaf-rosettes are ever-grey throughout the winter, and can form a neat edging along a path, but it should be remembered that the plant, when it flowers, will be almost two feet (61cm) high. Slugs do not touch it, so I am able to grow it in quantity.

25 June

To my delight I have just noticed that the Dragon Arum (*Dracunculus vulgaris*) has a single flowering spathe like a tightly rolled pale green umbrella. This is just beginning to darken and the sinister crimson edge is a herald of the startingly smelly plum-purple flower that is to be. Most people detest it, but I have great affection for the stronger characters of the garden, and a character this plant most certainly is. It is in flower for only three (sunny) days at the most, during which time it is pollinated by bluebottles and blowflies. The plant reeks of carrion, and passing downwind of it is an experience that is academically interesting rather than pleasant, particularly as at the height of its brief glory it is surrounded by a buzzing swarm of all the nastier species of insect. As soon as their task of fertilizing the spadix is done the flower withers and dies, though a fine knob of green berries should appear in the early autumn.

Pinks

Rose Campion

27 *June*

The wild yellow Irises (*Iris pseudacorus*) in the pond are coming out one by one and the flowers open very quickly, sometimes in the space of an hour on a warm day. These Irises are so obliging: they grow best in shallow water, but they will also do almost as well in a border, though they must have sun and will naturally appreciate copious watering. Their seed-heads are shiny, fat, green and interesting, and in late autumn, when these have fulfilled their purpose and have discharged their contents, the tripartite case splits and curls back to form an ever more interesting and long-lasting 'dried' plant for winter decoration.

28 *June*

Tall 'William Lobb' on the pergola is in flower, and it is just as interesting seen from the back as from the front with its heavily 'mossed' calyx and stem. There are tiny thorns among that gentle-seeming moss, so beware. The old Apothecary's Rose, once much used in medicine, has bright pink flowers of a very unusual colour which, when closely examined, will be seen to have petals that are delicately veined all over in a darker pink. Old roses were never a true red – this colour was not bred into the rose-spectrum until more modern times. What medieval poets called a 'red' rose was unknown in former days and was, at its darkest, a deep pink or cerise, probably very similar to the colour of *Rosa gallica officinalis* – the Apothecary's Rose, which was imported from France. Rose petals were used as a base for syrups, they were crystallized, infused, made into a 'honey' for sore throats, added to vinegar for headaches and even distilled into liqueurs. They were made into creams, pomades and lotions, and rose-water has been used for hundreds of years as a light and delicate perfume.

The Damask Rose 'Ispahan' is producing its characteristic and very sweetly scented flowers which will keep coming for almost six weeks now. I say 'characteristic' because the outer petals of this rose curve backwards against the stem, and this is often a good way to recognize the species even if the variety is unfamiliar.

29 *June*

June, that month of roses, is nearly over now, but as today is my birthday I have picked a great basket of them, lingering and looking, sniffing and smelling and making resolutions to care for them all a great deal better next year. I can, of course, begin the care this season with more regular spraying. This has been the worst year ever for black spot, that scourge of the genus rosa.

There are Pinks a-plenty in bloom and it is such a comfort to know that they are so easy to propagate, either with 'pipings' pulled cleanly from a non-flowering stem, or actual cuttings. Both should be placed round the edge of a clay pot in a compost of half and half peat to silver sand. There is not much nourishment in this, so as soon as the cuttings have rooted they should be transplanted into a more substantial mixture, though they still like this to have a high proportion of sand. (*Never* use builder's sand – it is only for builders.) I am very pleased to have grown the rare Cheddar Pink (*Dianthus gratianopolitanus*) from seed this year, and shall try to maintain a clump of them in the rock garden from now on.

Never assume that your fine old clump of the delicious 'Mrs Sinkins' that has been flowering so well for so many years will continue so to do. I was told of a very famous border of these sweetly scented old pinks that just died away in the early spring of this year for no apparent reason. So take plenty of cuttings in good time, remembering that they make nice hummocks of silver grey in the winter garden.

The plague of my June garden is *Geum urbanum* or Wood Avens. This is a wild flower that has shiny and interesting evergreen leaves which look as though they are something rather special, but when the tiny yellow flowers come in June and July, they are so small across – half an inch (1.25cm) – as to be a real disappointment. The plant's survival is ensured by hooked seeds that transfer themselves with easy alacrity to clothing and cat's fur, thus ensuring a fine new plant wherever they eventually fall. These come up in cracks in the paving and side by side with worthier plants in the rock gardens whom they starve of nourishment – having by far the stronger personality. Wood Avens thrives best in dampish places, and the better the soil the better the plant.

Rose Guinee

Opium Poppy

1 July

The last few days have been occupied with useful tidyings-up in the garden, tying and staking the July-heavy flowers and unwinding Bindweed. This is not a job to be done in a hurry, because pulling it straight off a plant will strip this of leaves and flowers as well. My method is to locate the exit point of the double stems from the ground and cut them through with scissors. Then I dig these up, and *that* plant will never grow again. Next, the twining stems are snipped every six inches or so up the host plant, and the strangling Bindweed can then be gently teased away in short sections, doing minimal damage to leaves and flowers. I filled two barrows full of these noxious snippings, and these I will burn when the weather changes, because I dare not light a bonfire while the grass is so dry in the field.

Some parts of the garden are looking quite successful, and one such is seen as the visitor rounds the corner of the cottage to go down the path to the studio. There is a very old semi-circular stone trough on the corner there which is full of *Nemesia* just coming into colourful bloom. This jolly brightness is backed by the tall magenta flowers and silver stems and leaves of Rose Campion (*Lychnis coronaria*). Beside this is a good patch of the blue Jacob's Ladder (*Polemonium caeruleum*) and beyond that is a purple-flowered *Tradescantia virginiana* or Spiderwort. All this, with the rose 'Eyepaint' and the Fuchsia rising above, make a close-growing mass of colour that is continued by the three earthenware bread-crocks on the other side full of bright Pelargoniums and Lobelia.

Three kinds and colours of Canterbury Bells (*Campanula medium*) are out a little further along, and these biennial plants are well worth growing. Other old fashioned biennials are Sweet Williams (*Dianthus barbatus*), Evening Primrose (*Oenothera biennis*), Honesty (*Lunaria biennis*) and of course the always popular Wallflower, usually treated as a biennial but in reality a short-lived perennial. If there is a small patch of ground in the vegetable garden where the plants can be set out in a row to grow on through their first year, they will appreciate the fine tilth of this usually well-raked and fertilized part of the garden. Looking after a vegetable garden is so easy: all that shouldn't be there is so easily recognizable, and everything else is in neat rows, making maintenance a very simple job compared with the care of a herbaceous border intermixed with roses, shrubs, bulbs, rhizomes and corms.

Sweet William

The wild Cornflowers are just coming out, but I cannot at the moment see any difference between them and the garden variety. They look most attractive in the wild flower bed, with the bright cerise flowers of the now-rare Corncockle (*Lychnis githago*) just in front of them, but this pleasing colour contrast is quite spoiled by the jolly orange-tawny dandelions of *Pilosella auranticum*, commonly called 'Fox and Cubs'. This is a rather uncommon member of the gigantic Hawkweed family, most of whose members look so alike. Pilosella is very different in its coloration, being the only member of the family to have orange flowers. Pilosella propagates itself most vigorously by means of stoloniferous runners, producing small new offsets a-plenty. It looks very well when grown among orange poppies.

Wild Honeysuckle (*Lonicera periclymenum*) scrambles along the fence here from one end, and its sweet scent mingles in the air with that of the roses and the Philadelphus. I have a wild rose that was the stock of some forgotten garden graft, and this provides me with the delicate flowers that are so characteristic of our summer hedges. The branches of wild roses have a definite arching form which is very recognizable, even when walking along a country lane in the dusk of a summer evening.

7 July

More and different roses are out and 'Mermaid' is early this year. What a lovely rose this is, with its large single flowers whose petals curl under in a very characteristic way. The golden stamens remain after the petals have tidily fallen and this is another of its pleasing ways. 'Mermaid' is a little tender, and prefers to grow on a South- or West-facing wall where it can enjoy more warmth. It dislikes being moved, and if possible, plants on their own roots should be obtained as these will last far longer. It is often in flower last of all, and is semi-evergreen in mild counties in a sheltered position.

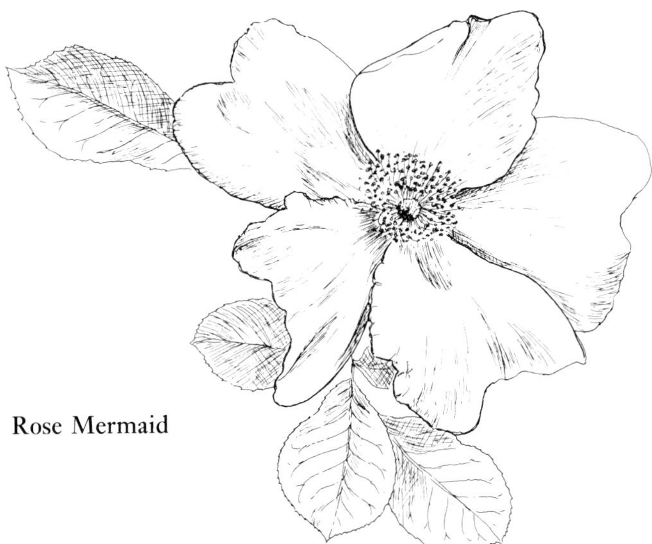

Rose Mermaid

Lilies scent the garden, and these bulbs have to be treated with care when they are being handled in the winter. I have a clump of Madonna Lilies (*Lilium candidum*) that is just coming into bloom. These are the only lilies that should be planted with their 'noses' just above the surface of the soil. They should not be disturbed if they are doing well, and they need a position in full sun. Madonna Lilies are more lime-tolerant than most other lilies, and will often send up a winter rosette of leaves which is very considerate of them, because this will indicate exactly where the bulbs are so they are less likely to be damaged by a carelessly wielded fork. They are said to be carriers of several Lily-diseases, so Lily-growers are not fond of them, and if they grow them at all, they do so in strictly segregated areas to prevent their other stock from being infected. As I am grateful for any flowers that any of my Lilies give me, I do my best to site them where they will be most contented, and fortunately these positions are all well separated from each other.

Lilium Royal Gold

8 July

The *Cistus ladanifer* is a mass of bloom at the end of the rose bed on the top lawn. This is a half-hardy evergreen shrub which I did not lose in the bad winters, much to my surprise. When it is a good year, as now, it is completely covered each day with fresh new white flowers with a maroon blotch in the centre. This is a Mediterranean shrub and should properly be planted in a sheltered situation.

14 July

I rose very early today so that I could have a quiet walk round the dewy garden before going off for the day. Amusingly, I was up and dressed before the Morning Glories, whose pleated trumpets were only just beginning to unfurl as the bright rays of the early morning sun fell upon them. These are lovely things to plant with bright pink Pelargoniums in hanging baskets and they trail and twine charmingly among the ivy-leaved varieties. The flowers are always over by midday and the afternoon visitors never see them. The leaves of the Morning Glory look very like those of its relative the Bindweed (*Calystegia sepium*), though the leaves of Ipomoea are thicker and rougher to the touch. But to the chance visitor they are so similar that I have more than once had to arrest the well-meaning hand that was about to pluck out the offending tendrils. If the flowers are out there is no problem, but in the afternoon when they are over, or on a dull day, they are often at considerable hazard, particularly as the garden this year has more than its share of this strangling weed.

In the pond the lilies are out, following the sun all day. The pond is a little congested this year because in the winter I gratefully accepted the gift of a large Water-lily from a friend and it has more than covered its allotted corner and is now larger than large. I have just seen another frog, which certainly confirms that the garden – particularly around the pond – is a suitable habitat for this increasingly scarce reptile.

Canterbury Bell

15 July

On the fence where the variegated Ivy 'Gloire de Marengo' used to grow until the successive bad winters of 1977 and 1978 killed it (I am *so* glad that I took those cuttings) there is a mounding exuberance of Convolvulus (*Calystegia sepium*). Not many people stop to look at Convolvulus without cursing, because it is usually busy choking the life out of choicer plants; I call it Convolvulus when I am admiring it and Bindweed when I am wrenching it out of the soil, but it *is* beautiful, and it is fascinating to stand and watch the wild bees entering the pure white trumpets for their daily bread. Wild bees begin working far earlier in the day than hive bees – I have seen the wild ones busy at 5 am on a June morning, whereas the hive bees are still asleep, or at least just yawning and stretching.

Cornflower

Convolvulus stems usually grow in pairs or even twisted ropes and they *always* twiddle in an anticlockwise direction, but you must look down on it to discern this properly, otherwise the stems appear to be climbing from left to right. An easy, if untidy way of making Convolvulus unhappy is to untwiddle it and leave it lying on the path. If the cellular structure is damaged in this fashion – bending the stems in the opposite way to that in which they have been growing – the Convolvulus-Bindweed will die, though it will probably take a long and yellowing time about it. Even Tennyson had trouble with the plant, writing this cumbersome couplet as follows:

The lustre of the long convolvuluses
That coil'd around the stately stems

There are many plants that need a little bit of stonework, brickwork or some tasteful concrete to keep them within bounds. Montbretia (though it has the newer and grander name of *Crocosmia*) and the wild Silverweed formerly called Goose-Grey or Midsummer Silver, are two such. What a lovely plant this last one is, each leaf being made up of a variable number of 'feathers' which are a fresh green on the top and a shimmering silver beneath. This silver shows up on a windy day in the country when the breeze blows along a country road or field path, and the Midsummer Silver shimmers and ripples like river water. This plant is a determined survivor, propagating itself purposefully with runners or stolons equipped with small tufts of rooted leaves. If it is planted in a pocket of soil with paving all round it for several yards, it cannot escape to colonize the area.

The wasps are beginning to be noticeable, and in hot summers they seem to spend most of the day nibbling away at the teak garden chairs which we were advised to paint with teak oil, and never did because they looked so new and painfully raw at the time. Now all the furniture has a charmingly weathered appearance much appreciated by the wasps, who sit in the sun and spend their days removing slivers of my expensive teak to make their silvery nests. It is too late now to paint the seats and I can actually hear the wasps' mandibles scraping away at the table where I am sitting to write these notes.

By the pond there is some grass with green and white striped leaves called Gardener's Garters (*Phalaris arundinacea variegata*). The cats love eating it in the spring, but I only see them actually doing this when I am taking people round the garden and the cats are vying with my visitors for attention. Sometimes they manage to eat it faster than it can grow, but it always catches up later in the year. My Gardener's Garters need to be enclosed in stone or concrete, or they will march charmingly but relentlessly all over everything in their path, so I have moved the clumps to prison-pockets in the various rock gardens where they cannot escape. One clump shows up particularly well because it is planted against the sombre green of a tall thin Juniper.

I am not as attracted by variegated leaves as some gardeners are, and a little variegation with me goes a long way. A useful list would include Ivy, Gardener's Garters, Hosta, Strawberry, Hebe, Periwinkle, *Aucuba*, *Galeobdolon*, *Eleagnus*, Holly 'Silver Queen' and *Cornus elegantissima.* These are a constant delight to me, and it is a small enough population in the garden, when spread about, not to dominate the surrounding greenery nor make one feel that everything is a little unwell.

The cottage

Wand Flower

20 *July*

A warm, sunny day with a light breeze. I had hoped for some rain for the garden and had been planning to spend the day in the greenhouse, where the Cathedral Bells (*Cobaea scandens*) have been ramping over the Cymbidium, the Jasmine and the Oleander.

The Cobaea, which has grown from a single seed given to me last year, began in June to produce interesting six-sided buds that are in reality the calyx. The buds grew larger and flowers like Canterbury Bells form to open as a pleasing pale green, remaining so for a day. Then they become tinged with mauve and by the end of the second day the flowers are a rich purple. They last one more day and then fall to the floor, but there are many more to come. Cobaea will grow quite well in the open air against a warm wall in a hot summer, though it will never have the luxuriance that it has under glass.

The Oleander is in full flower now and many legends surround this very typical and beautiful Mediterranean shrub. It is said that the Borgias had drinking cups made from the wood and as every part of the shrub is poisonous there could be but one end for the unfortunate who used such a cup.

24 *July*

The glaucous green of Opium Poppy leaves (*Papaver somniferum*) seems to be everywhere. These are very good things to have in the July borders, because they hybridize all the time, sometimes producing astonishing flowers that resemble Peonies in both colour and appearance. One year I had a whole tract of them in the field, but a wheedling flower-arranger came along for the dried heads and I forgot to take any seed. Since then the population in the garden dwindled almost to nothing, but by leaving what few I had where they were and scattering the seeds every year the numbers are coming back again. Nothing much will happen until late spring, but one day you will see thousands of seedling poppies, small as a finger-nail, all over the seeded area. Thin out the unwanted ones and leave the rest to grow. The small flat leaf-rosettes can be moved at this time by taking up a large trowel of soil with them, but later on they grow long thin tap-roots that will not tolerate transplanting, so one has to live with them wherever they have popped up if one wants the seeds for the following year. I am hoping for some more of the wonderful doubly-double crimson ones again, so I am persevering.

Gardener's Garters

Lilium pyrenaicum

25 July, 5 am

I woke early and had no desire to go back to sleep, so with tea-cup in hand I wandered round the garden to see how things were doing, accompanied by the cats who are always glad of company at odd hours. The Wand-flowers, sometimes called 'Angel's Fishing Rods' (*Diarama pulcherrimum*), are in bloom by the pond. These very lovely plants look their best when planted near water – they seem to like to look at their own reflections. When acquiring this plant, careful thought should be given to its permanent siting, because, like *Iris unguicularis*, it detests being transplanted and may die to spite you. It should be thought about, bought and planted, and *never* thereafter moved. Eventually you will have a gigantic clump of sharp-edged rushy leaves from which will grow as many as two dozen wands of magenta flowers, always a-tremble even when there is no breeze whatsoever.

30 July

This is the time of year when most gardens look summer-tired. The best of the roses are over or are drawing breath for a later effort. There should be in all the best-planned gardens a sufficiency of flowering plants for this time of year, because otherwise the garden seems suddenly to be a symphony in green. Pansies are very useful, but one must dead-head them regularly and they like a liquid feed once a fortnight. Marguerites (*Chrysanthemum maximum*) are marvellous and can be relied upon to keep going for about five weeks.

A weed of the July garden is that cunning nuisance the Broad-leaved Willow Herb (*Epilobium montanum*), whose shiny, neat leaf-rosettes should always have been twitched out in early spring. Those that were missed then have been growing secretly among all the other growth of the border and it is now that it reasserts itself, peeping out from the centre of an otherwise perfect clump of Larkspurs, or already shedding its seeds among the delicate Campanulas in the rockery. Its flowers are small and pale, its habit of growth is inconspicuous, and its legion seeds are all winged. No matter how fiercely I pounce on every plant, more will float over the fence on the prevailing breeze.

1 August

I am always covetous of Geraniums, or, as they should more properly be called, Pelargoniums. True Geraniums are the perennial herbaceous plants that are (usually) hardy enough to require no attention whatsoever except a little largesse from the fertilizer-barrow when it does its rounds late in the year. Pelargoniums, on the other hand, are nothing but a nuisance and I love them dearly. They fill my greenhouse in winter almost to the exclusion of everything else, so much so that I am thinking of boarding out the larger tender plants and shrubs such as the *Hedychium gardneranum*, the *Lippia citriodora* and the Oleander.

For several hundred years Pelargoniums have been grown by cottagers on sunny window-sills, even through the period of Victorian carpet bedding when similar plants were regimentally planted out for this very fashionable 'look' which, alas, helped to hasten the end of the far more interesting herbaceous border. Pelargoniums have never lost their popularity, because all they need is a sunny position and a little shelter, and they will then give of their best, producing long-lasting trusses of brilliant flowers which last for weeks. I change the soil in my tubs and pots once a year incorporating silver sand, peat and bonemeal with freshly sifted soil from the field. This simple mix seems to suit them well, and though they are somewhat etiolated after their winter spent under the staging in the greenhouse, they soon plump out and grow new leaves and flowering stems after the application of a little weak liquid manure.

The miniature Pelargoniums are more demanding of ideal conditions than the taller varieties and in a bad year they do not do well and have fewer flowers. I tried mine outside last summer (which was an unusually rainy one) thinking that they might like a change from their cosseted existence in the greenhouse, but they did not thrive, so I soon brought them in again and within five weeks they had recovered from the rigours of the great outdoors and were covered in bloom once more.

Pelargonium Mrs Henry Cox

4 August

The days are very hot and humid, and I have a strong disinclination for work of any kind. It is turning out to be a most excellent summer, and the shrubs are putting on plenty of woody growth. In fact, everything has put on plenty of growth in every direction and seems to be joining hands all along the borders.

The Lavender (*Lavandula spica*) at the corner of the cottage is particularly good this year, and is a rest stop for all the butterflies that pass through the garden. Lavender should always be planted where it can be brushed against in passing, for the pure pleasure of it, and all that the bushes need is a situation in full sun. If the flowers are wanted for sachets and sweet bags the stems should be picked when the 'lavender' colour is just beginning to show and before the flowers have opened. The stems should be tied into a bunch and hung, flowers downward, in a cool airy place until they are dry. The shrubs have a tendency to grow tall and leggy with age, and if planted as a hedge, gaps seem to appear at the base of the shrub after about five years or so (this tendency is always exacerbated by the animals of the household, who will have made their own short cuts in the most sensible though conspicuous places). When the plants become shaggy and uneven in height they can be removed, fresh soil brought in and new bushes planted. Cuttings can be taken from ripe non-flowering shoots, and these should be put into a mixture of half peat and half sand and kept in a cold frame or unheated greenhouse throughout their first winter.

Buddleia

Elecampane

The Romneya is out and is the most striking feature of the August garden. I think that a combination of several things has made it more magnificent than ever: the mildness of the winter months (few of its branches were frosted as they have been in previous years); its own maturity here, the plant being six years in the garden; the good summer that we are having, with a long succession of warm sunny days; and a warm south-facing position with a low wall behind it. There must be as many as twenty of the huge white Poppy-flowers in bloom at the same time which have been opening at regular intervals over the last fortnight. They have a curious, faintly narcotic and rather unpleasant scent.

5 *August*

Inula helenium is an ancient cough-cure, though my heart simply would not allow me to dig it up to concoct the remedy from its roots, the part most generally used. Inula, or Elecampane as it is more often called, is a tall-growing shaggy flowered yellow Daisy, much beloved by the Small Tortoiseshell butterflies who positively rock about on their dinner-tables in their ecstasies over the quality of its nectar. I watch them with amusement from my place at the drawing board – their rather undignified antics can be comfortably observed because we are all at the same level. Sometimes, overcome by the effect of their own gluttony, they fall over sideways. The butterflies will visit the Elecampane until the end of the month, when the last of the blooms will be over; this is an excellent late-summer plant to grow for them, as are *Solidago spp* and the old-fashioned Michaelmas Daisy (*Aster Spp*), of which the pink-flowering kinds are the best.

6 August, 5 am

The crescent moon still sits in the sky accompanied by one or two bright stars. A dawn breeze shivers in the bamboos, though dawn itself has only just begun to lighten the sky in the east, and the sky in the west is still night-dark. I am walking in the garden at this time in the morning in my usual insomniac way, curious to see what difference the night makes to the flowers and leaves, and as it is still dark I have a torch and three interested cats for company.

Naturally, the trumpets of the Convolvulus-flowers on the fence are closed against the cool summer night, like a collection of neatly-furled garden-party parasols. All the leaves of the Nasturtiums hang perpendicularly, presenting less surface to the air; by breakfast-time, in the first rays of the sun, they will have straightened up and flattened out, and their round leaf-plates will be horizontal once more.

But attention is diverted from the Nasturtiums by a whistling postman who is coming along the road on his bicycle to work; its light is brighter than the tired moon. How loud and cheerful – and tuneless! – is his whistle, as he rides carelessly in the middle of the empty road, quite unaware of me (in my dressing gown and grass-wet slippers) and the companion cats behind the vulgar Leylandii hedge. On one of the low walls beneath the skirts of the hedge there is an obstinate clump of the pink flowered *Oxalis floribunda*, an all-embracing name for any or all of the four species of the commoner garden Oxalis: *O. rosea*, *O. rubra*, *O. articulata*, *O. lasiandra*. Its leaves hang in tight pleats, again to present as little surface as possible to the coolness of the night. This is a plant much hated by proper gardeners because it spreads so rapidly, though it is quite taken for granted by sensible folk with cottage gardens because it acts as a useful barometer – the flowers close quickly with the change of barometric pressure, and they do not open on dull days.

Round at the back of the house I can only shine the torch-beam up at the three tall annual Sunflowers (*Helianthus annua*). These quick-growing and heavy-headed plants should be planted facing towards the south, and they can then be watched through the day as they follow the sun on its journey through

Pelargonium Paul Crampel

the heavens. At night their round and cheerful faces look towards the western sky as the sun sinks towards the horizon, but during the night they turn slowly back again to face the east once more to greet the sun after whom they were named. As it is so nearly sunrise they are almost there, rather unevenly peering round the corner of the cottage; by sunrise they will be perfectly in position. I should mention that after sunset they turn back the same way they turned during the day, not spirally. If they did, each would be an incredible giant green corkscrew, with as many turns in it as the sunrises that the flowers had seen.

The cats accompany me closely as I poke about with my torch and a snatched cane in the dark and dewy garden; it is not affection, or surprises or even fear – just feline practicality. 'As you're up', they are saying, 'what about breakfast?'

14 August

I have just seen a late female Brimstone butterfly pugnaciously doing battle with a Large White over the same flower, *Ligularia* 'Desdemona'. Unfortunately the Brimstone lost interest and it was the Large White that settled to feed on the ragged orange daisies. The Brimstone would have been aesthetically more pleasing.

Now is the time to enjoy one's garden. Gardens are for sitting and dreaming in, for marvelling and admiration, for the healing of sick souls and wounded spirits, and for contented silence with a loved one at dusk. What has been done and planned so much earlier in the year, or in the autumn before, is taking place now and it is either a gratifying success or a barren failure. In a good year the successes are often so successful as to outweight the failures. The first of the *Cyclamen neapolitanum* flowers are out on the lawn under the old apple tree, with many more flower buds appearing from the bare ground. As yet there are no leaves, but the charmingly marbled foliage will start to appear in about a month's time. If these Cyclamen are happy, they should be left to increase and multiply. When the flower is over the petals wither and the seed forms at the end of the spiralling stem. In time the stem will bend to the ground and the seed will be 'planted' – eventually to grow into another corm. The corms of *C. coum* root from the middle of the underside and the corms of *C. neapolitanum*, which in flower is very similar, root from the *upper* part of the corm.

As these two delightful species are so similar, and the flowering periods overlap (*coum* flowers from winter to spring and *neapolitanum* from July to November) sometimes the only way to tell them apart is to dig them up, which they could tolerate if one could leave the soil-ball intact around them, but this has to be pulled away to see just exactly where the roots are coming from. Never buy these forms of Cyclamen as corms – they are exceedingly difficult to start into growth, and, in any case, with no roots at all and little to show where they were, it is impossible to know which way up to plant them.

Hedychium Garderianum

Cyclamen persicum, which is the 'florist's Cyclamen', is so devastatingly beautiful as a gift at Christmas time but *so* difficult to keep healthy and happy afterwards. Mine has suffered at least two changes of living temperature and it can't abide this. If you can keep it going until the last of the flowers are over, let it spend the summer in a shady place in the garden, where it can recover from your ministrations, and you can then learn to look after it for the following winter's flowers.

Hedychium gardneranum is at last in flower, quite justifying its winter stay in the overcrowded greenhouse. This is a tender plant that is closely related to true ginger which seldom flowers. Hedychium will oblige every year if it is kept in the equivalent of jungle conditions – semi-shade and high humidity. It can be stood outside in such a summer as this one, as long as the pot is in the shade. It needs plenty of liquid manure while growing, and can be safely stood in warm water if tropical water plants are being grown. If it is being grown in a pot, it needs to be watered at least three times a day, particularly when the flower-buds can be seen to have formed. The flowers are heavily perfumed and two or three of these handsome spikes are very imposing. Later on, equally interesting seed-heads form which will be quickly snapped up by any flower arranger worthy of the name.

18 August

Fruit is beginning to ripen. The peach tree has its first fruit – three heavily protected peaches which will taste infinitely better than anything one can buy. The problem is always – when to pick? Probably like apples, when the fruit falls off in one's caressing hand.

20 August

How quickly the year is passing. The grasses are still green in the field, though not for much longer. Grasses are the most exquisite things, full of rippling movement as the wind swoops down the side of a hill – from a comfortable seat on an opposite slope one can see exactly where the invisible wind is.

21 August

In the greenhouse the Bougainvillea is flowering, which I always feel is something of a triumph. This tough shrub of hotter lands does not like our cloud-layer here and needs a warm place on the south side of a heated greenhouse if it is even to think of flowering at all. As mine is still in a (large) pot it is all right for perhaps one more year, but if it continues to grow at the rate it has this season, well, it will have to be pruned like any Mediterranean wall shrub.

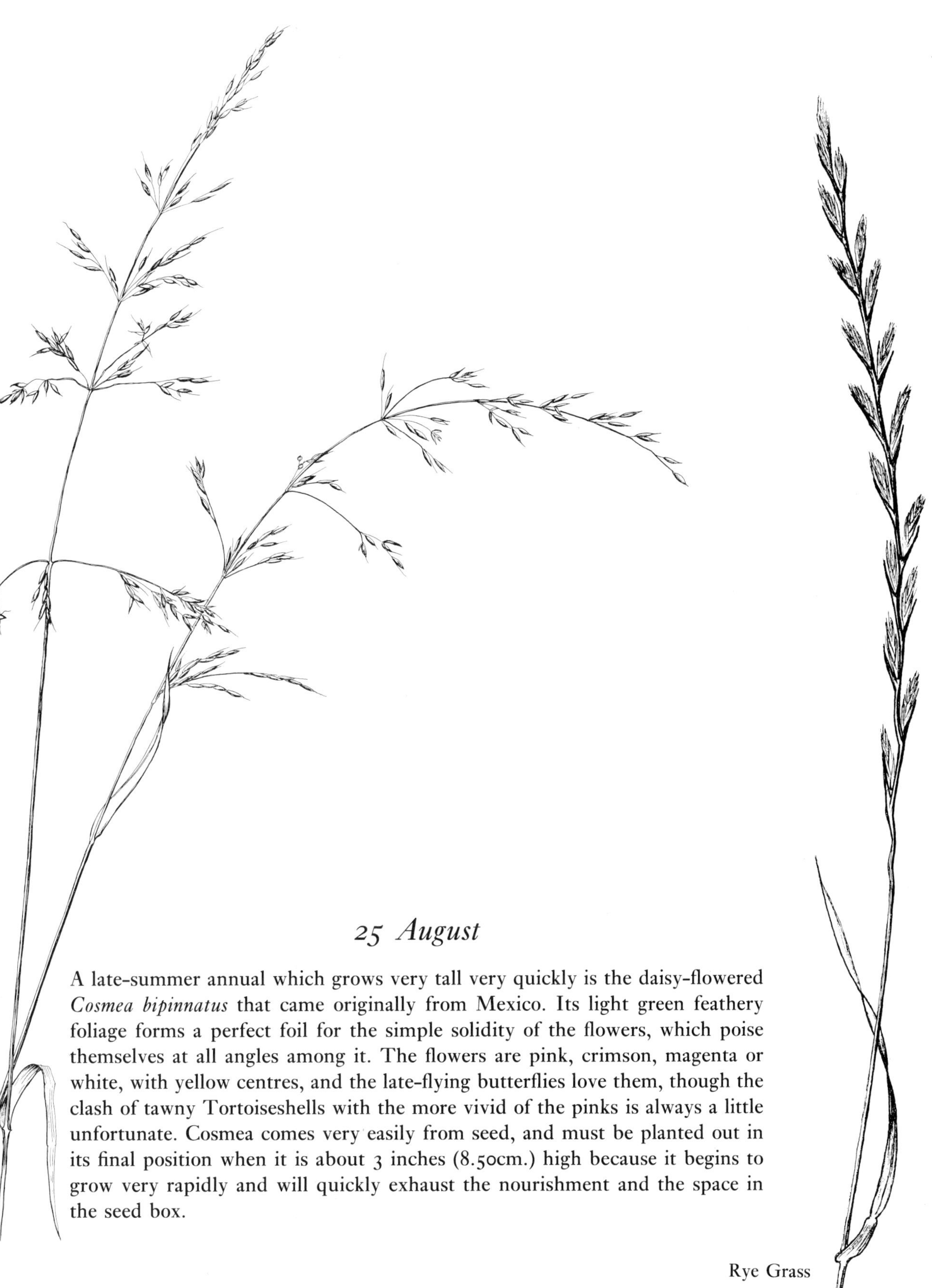

25 August

A late-summer annual which grows very tall very quickly is the daisy-flowered *Cosmea bipinnatus* that came originally from Mexico. Its light green feathery foliage forms a perfect foil for the simple solidity of the flowers, which poise themselves at all angles among it. The flowers are pink, crimson, magenta or white, with yellow centres, and the late-flying butterflies love them, though the clash of tawny Tortoiseshells with the more vivid of the pinks is always a little unfortunate. Cosmea comes very easily from seed, and must be planted out in its final position when it is about 3 inches (8.50cm.) high because it begins to grow very rapidly and will quickly exhaust the nourishment and the space in the seed box.

Rye Grass

28 August

This is the time of year to take as many cuttings as possible. Certain plants come very easily from cuttings if these are taken in the right way at the right time of year and if they are planted in the right compost. The weather has been very warm and humid for several days now, with light rainfall in the mornings. This is quite perfect for those cuttings that are left outside, and all of them have to be looked at several times a day to make sure that the exceptional temperatures – often 80°F (25°C) by mid-afternoon – have not dried out the pots. I sprinkle them all lightly with the last of the rainwater at midday and at about five pm and find that this helps them to root more quickly.

Certain plants need heat to 'strike' and others do not, and many need the whole winter to form roots. Several plants in the garden such as the Romneya, the Akebia, and a particularly vicious briar called *Rubus ulmifolius bellidiflorus* that is producing its delightful puffs of very double pale pink flowers this month, need to be layered. One provides pots of various sizes with various composts in them and then the chosen branch, runner or cane is pegged firmly into place so that the roots, when they form, will have a comfortable bed in which to begin life. I peg the growth down twice: once very strongly and deeply into the ground by the pot, and again in the pot itself, because no matter how out-of-the-way the pots are the whole arrangement is very easily disturbed. The enormously long canes of the Rubus should yield me at least three new plants each (these are very useful for hedging, though one must not cut off the flower buds). If the stem is woody I slice into it on the underside with a clean sharp knife and dust the cut with rooting powder.

Nasturtium

Cosmea

30 August

The Agapanthus flowers are very handsome in their tubs outside the two front doors (once upon a time, the cottage was two dwellings). I overwintered these very heavy stone tubs in the greenhouse for several years, but each spring I had to cast about for two simultaneously strong and willing 'lifters' to carry the pots up through the garden into their summer homes. Each year I found it more and more of a nuisance, so last year I left them out all the winter and am rewarded by the same number of flower-stems as usual – three per pot. There must be a moral here somewhere.

Agapanthus is a greedy creature, and one can almost see it gulping at the liquid fertilizer. Eventually the plants will have to be split up, but I am deferring this for yet another year. When the necessity is really imminent, the job will have to be done in early spring, after the frosts have left the garden, with two forks back to back in order to split the huge and heavy roots apart. The plants will take a year to recover but should flower the following summer if they are planted in a hot and sheltered position. The seed-heads are large and striking, and if not appropriated by someone for a vase, the seeds can be dried and planted and will produce small plants that can be grown on in pots in a cold frame.

The weed of almost any month in this garden is the obnoxious, choking, smothering, detestable Ground Elder or Bishop Weed (*Aegopodium podagraria*). This hateful plant was introduced by the monks of long ago as a herbal remedy to soothe the pains of gout, and since gout was and is the result of a lifetime of tippling, those old monasteries must have been quite cheerful places, though damp. Ground Elder escaped under the walls to populate our gardens, and lucky is he who has never seen it. I have been struggling with it for seven years, and it is as healthy, as green, as sturdy and probably more vigorous than when I began my attempts at eradication. In a garden with shrubs and Ground Elder one can never get rid of it completely, because this noxious plant of the running roots will nestle among those of the shrubs for protection and the only way of eradicating it is to dig it up, shrub and all. Most of my shrubs are now approaching maturity, so this is no longer possible, but I spend many back-breaking hours carefully lifting up herbaceous plants and unthreading the clearly recognizable roots of the Ground Elder from among the roots of the protecting perennial. This evil weed will wriggle under a properly laid path and bob up on the other side, ready and eager to colonize new territory.

When attempting to clear a flower bed of this vegetable villain, the most thorough way is to choose a day immediately after rain when the soil will be damp, and then to dig up everything in the bed and sort out the roots. The proper tenants can be put back as quickly as possible, and because of the moist soil they will suffer little harm. Do not, however, move Peonies, and Agapanthus resent any upheaval whatsoever. Before the plants are put back, the soil can be sifted, if the area is not too large, and this will catch the little broken roots of the Ground Elder, which when left in the soil will take a deep breath and look around them, pleased as Punch at all the spacious new accommodation. On no account put any of these roots in the compost heap – they will not break down, and even if they do, some will escape to start up a new colony. Ground Elder likes to grow along the foundations of walls, and one can often drag out great hanks of seemingly endless root, which is temporarily encouraging.

Agapanthus

3 September

The weather is still very warm, but the garden is tired, the bright greens of midsummer are beginning to fade and some of the herbaceous plants look a sad sight, flopping and dropping about and needing either string or shears. *Tradescantia virginiana* is one such, and on cutting away the summer stems one can see next year's growth already peeping above the ground. This is what is so heartening about a garden – there is no definite time when one can say 'This is the end of the year, it is winter, nothing is growing'. There is never an end to the slowly revolving seasons that each plant has, and each season of each plant is slightly different, so there is always a time of surprise and *always* something happening.

To neglect a garden slightly is a very good thing. I say this, perhaps from necessity, but more because through leaving a part of the garden unweeded and untended, the most delightful surprises greet one when the overhanging tangle

Clematis orientalis 'Lemon Peel'

of dead stems and dying leaves is lifted at this time of year. There, beneath all this natural protection, may be found one prize seedling of a plant not normally so inclined. Gardens that are constantly swept and scarified never have a chance to give things back.

8 September

The *Clematis orientalis* 'Lemon Peel' is always magnificent at this time of year, long after most of the others are just a muddle of seed-heads and fading leaves. The light-green lanterns that hang among the lushness of the foliage unfold their four 'petals' (Clematis is related to the Buttercup, and therefore has no real petals – these are developed sepals) and there is the flower, with the thickness of these 'petals' most exactly resembling the lemon peel for which they are named.

There are hundreds of buds still to open, and it would be interesting to see just how large an unpruned Clematis of this type would grow if left unchecked. This one of necessity has to be cut back so that we can go in and out of the shed, and on its other side it forms an archway at the corner of the cottage. From this particular point, long branches at least thirty feet in length climb and twine along the wire-netting that edges the thatch (to prevent the birds using it for easy nesting material in spring). I am often embarrassed by all this luxuriance, particularly when showing someone rather nice round the garden just after rain. It is amazing to find out just how much water is still trapped among the million Clematis leaves, needing but a touch and a careless brush to bring it all down in what seems like a bucketful on the innocent and undeserving visitor.

12 September

Vegetable flowers are very interesting, and seldom seen except on neglected allotments or in this garden – which often amounts to more or less the same thing. Bean flowers are most attractive, particularly to bees, and Runner Beans are worth growing for their flowers alone. Radishes have sprays of delicate pink, very typical crucifer flowers, among which interesting seed pods form. Carrots are particularly nice: they have a large white umbel which, as it ages, turns into a sort of green birdcage that stays in the same form right through the winter, and the sparkle of frost on the crisp brown 'cage' is certainly worth a carrot or two.

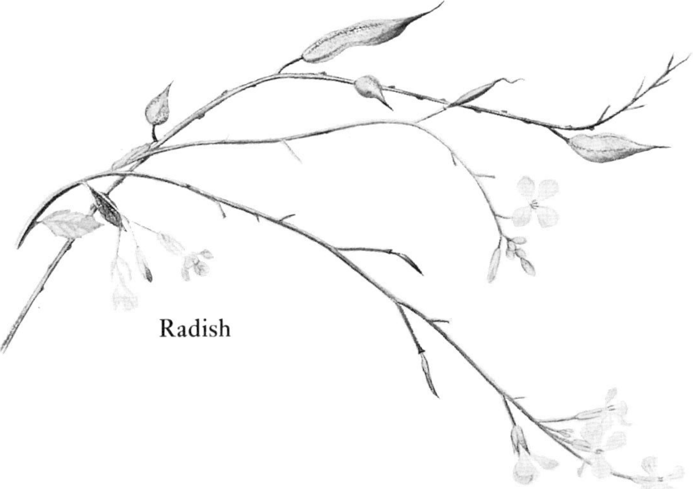

Radish

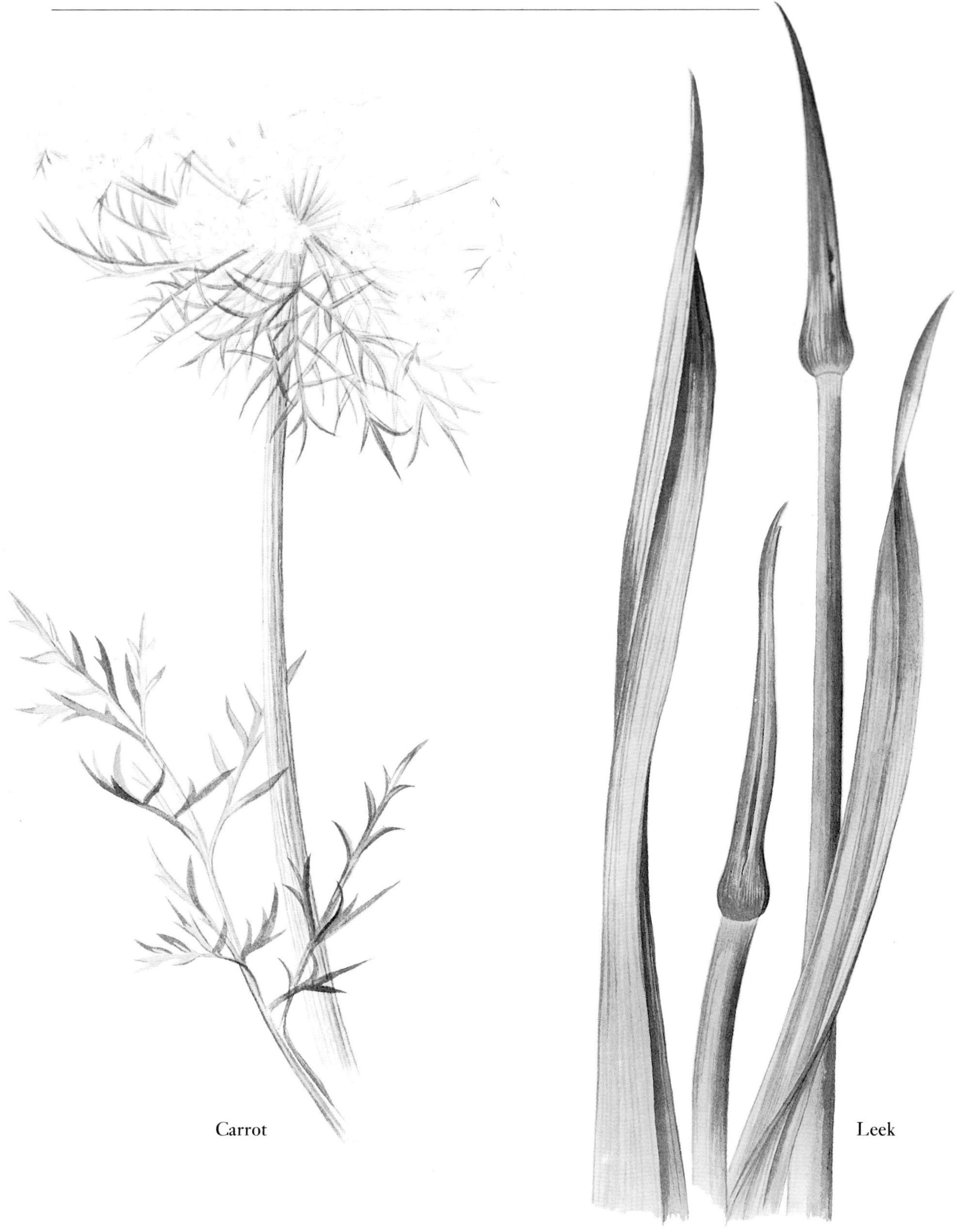

Carrot

Leek

Only the old-fashioned varieties do this prolifically; as a rule, the modern hybrids are shy to flower. Garlic is another most handsome plant when it condescends to set seed, and it has to be planted in the hottest, driest corner of the vegetable garden if this is to happen. The separate 'seeds' will all grow into new cloves for the following year. Leeks are very sculptural, if smelly, particularly if they can be caught just as their papery dunce caps split open to release the greenish-mauve flowers that form a perfect sphere. I often think that I will grow some Leeks as border 'Alliums', which of course they are. They would be a great deal cheaper to buy than pedigree bulbs, and I am quite sure that nobody would recognize them for what they are, particularly if there were several other varieties of Allium in the same part of the garden. There is the added advantage that Leeks can be timed to flower in late autumn, when all the other Alliums are long past their best.

Lettuce

Onions have a smaller flower on shorter, thicker stems and are not nearly so attractive. Potatoes have rather indeterminate flowers because their main reproduction takes place below ground, and they do not really need their blossoms. Peas are not particularly pretty but their pods are so pleasant and crisp to pop and they have such a fresh, clean green look to them. Lettuces are quite attractive when they have 'bolted', with their small bright yellow flowers that do not open on dull days.

Potato
Garlic
Onion

This is the fruitful time – the time of harvest, when all the seeds are forming, the wheat is whitening and the fruit is beginning to change colour. I have some clumps of corn in the field which I re-sow every year in case I should need to paint them. How very different they all are, and how essential they are to man. Wheat is stiff and pale when ripe, with almost no colour at all. Oats are graceful and tremble in the wind, and Barley is haphazard and whiskery. Rye is not often seen in this area because when grown it is as a fodder crop and is eaten long before it has a chance to form a proper head of grain.

Blackberries are ripening in the field and I suppose that one would not appreciate the fruit half as much if the briars had no thorns. The bushes in the field are getting larger and larger with the passing years, but they are the source of a tremendous quantity of particularly large fruit almost an inch across (2cm). I often feel that the briars must have begun life as neat rows of cultivated plants, but there is no trace of that neatness now. They are growing larger and wilder each season and will, as like as not, snatch back the half-filled fruit basket, which is one of the saddest things that can possibly happen when picking blackberries. There is no finding the cascade of ripeness down there in the thorny green depths, and one must start all over again.

Mulberry

Apple

14 September

In the rockery, a wasp's nest has formed very quickly. Strung above it is a small spider's web with Madame Spider sitting in wait in the centre of it. A wasp from the nest has flown into it and is struggling frantically to be free of the sticky threads, wings a-blur with vibration. The web is not really meant for such a large and vigorous insect, and the wasp is able to break free and fly off unsteadily, still bound about with spider-web. During the time that it was fighting its way back to freedom, another wasp flew slowly round it to see what was to do, but it did not do anything positive like stinging Madame Spider. Ah! While I watch, two more wasps have flown out of the nest and appear to be attacking Madame Spider, though with their biting, not stinging ends, and she is jounced about in the tattered remains of her web. Now the wasps have gone. Madame Spider would have built her web all unknowing in the night, and the web will not last much longer now because the wasps seem to be deliberately flying into the framework threads to break them.

Honeysuckle

16 September

The Passion Flower (*Passiflora caerulea*) has grown very well this year, and has reached up to tangle with the longest stems of the Clematis 'Lemon Peel' above it on the edge of the thatch. Passion Flowers will usually survive even the worst winters if they are planted against a south-facing wall, as this one is, though I did not have it during the harsh weather of 1977 and 1978. The variety *caerulea* is the one most generally seen, though it is not as hardy as 'Constance Elliott', which has ivory-white flowers. A mature plant will produce dozens of delicious golden fruit, but one likes to leave them on the 'vine' as long as possible because they look so attractive, like orange lanterns.

The Passion Flower is so called because all its parts symbolize the instruments of the Crucifixion. The leaf represents the spear, the five anthers are the five wounds of Christ, the tendrils are the cords and whips, the column of the ovary is the pillar of the cross, the three styles are the nails, the stamens are the hammers with which the cross was made, the filaments the crown of thorns, the calyx is the glory, the white petals are purity and the blue ones represent heaven.

All the fruit is beginning to ripen now. Apples, Pears, Elderberries, and all the Mulberry trees in the town are heavy with their particoloured fruits – some light red, some crimson and the best and most delicious are the darkest, often nearly black in colour.

Broad Bean

20 September

The aromatic Myrtle (*Myrtus communis*) is flowering away in its pot. This is a replacement shrub for the one that was lost in those freezing winters, and I am chary of planting it out lest I lose this one too. On the other hand, it is growing well and is now in my largest clay pot. The border on the south side of the house will have to be firmly rearranged this autumn and after another winter in the shelter of the warm greenhouse I will give it some of this precious wall-space. The Peach is taking up rather too much room for the ratio of peaches per square foot, so I think that I will make a present of it to someone who has a nice piece of unclothed south wall.

Pea

Fig

Aromatic scents in the garden are much rarer than sweet ones, and they make a pleasant change. *Choisya ternata* is a shrub that has deliciously scented flowers and unexpectedly pungent-smelling leaves. Marigolds (*Calendula officinalis*) have a medicinal smell, and are used as a remedy for healing small wounds without a scar. As a child I had a very bad cut on the sole of my foot, which to an active, tree-climbing, hill-walking, cliff-scrambling adolescent was a calamity beyond enduring. I knew a strange old lady who made equally strange cures from this and that plucked from the hedges and the then unpolluted fields. Unknown to my mother I cycled dangerously and painfully to her home for a daily application of her Marigold ointment, and daily I could both see and feel the wound healing cleanly and see the lessening of its extent. As my mother had been a nurse I was, to my way of thinking, being sensible in not telling her. She would never have understood.

Myrtle

The Dahlias are flowering again. Because of the gastropod problems I have almost given up trying to grow these useful late-summer flowers, but there is a patch of tubers that I leave in the ground and protect as much as possible with the poison pellets. As so often happens, they were a gift and I can only guess at their name. They are a dwarf variety and are a fine bright scarlet, which is most cheering among all the early autumn yellows.

Dahlia

The path by the pergola

I have a dread of being invaded by an exotic 'weed' that is the most invasive plant ever to have been carefully cultivated – to begin with. Japanese knotweed (*Polygonum cuspidatum*) is a tall herbaceous perennial that was imported as a curiosity from Japan in 1825. It took to our climate as a duck does to water and probably tunnelled its way out of its first greenhouse in a determined effort to escape. Since then it has spread throughout the kingdom, appearing at the corners of recreation grounds, in lay-bys, in car-parks and in almost any place where municipal efforts are not thorough enough to eradicate it.

It is huge and handsome, producing dainty trails of small white flowers, but these are the only dainty thing about it. It has jointed red-brown stems and leaves of a perfectly contrasting mid-green and is most attractive to look at, but . . . beware! It has the most tremendous root system ever, which can crack concrete as easily as you or I can crack an eggshell. It is capable of running along underground for yards and will cross beneath driveways to reappear as a huge thicket on the other side. The nearest patch of this fearsome plant is about ten yards from my back door, and as the sparrow flies, about five from the potting shed, and I would never be surprised to open the door one day and be greeted by a shedful of greenery. Polygonum dies down in the winter, and one may temporarily master it, but if you once have it you will be unlikely ever to be rid of it. As I have said, I like and admire it, because it is exceedingly handsome, but I am terrified of it because it is bigger and stronger than I am.

3 October

October – month of rosy apples and scarlet hips. Some of the colours of the seeds that ripen in the warmth are so startling as to seem artificial and I am thinking in particular of the Steep Holm Peony (*Paeonia mascula*), whose pink and black seed-head is as bright as a tropical flower. Peonies will grow from seed but often take about two years to germinate, so patience should be planted in the pot along with the precious seed. Peonies are usually divided rather than grown from seed, because they will take many years to come to flowering if grown in this way even in ideal conditions.

Hips of Dog Rose

Chinese Lanterns – the seed-cases of *Physalis franchetii* – are an autumn delight, and I am always happy to see them once more. Their papery fragility is part of their charm, and their bright colour gives a lift to an otherwise too-exquisite dried flower arrangement in too many subtleties of brown and beige. The plants come easily from seed sown in spring, and grow very quickly. Those folk who despise them say that they are invasive, but I am always grateful for plants that can be positively counted on to be greedy for growing and garden-space, for one knows where one is and can act accordingly. The flowers are inconspicuous and un-memorable – similar to those of the Potato, to which the plant is closely related. It is therefore poisonous, so the round seeds that rattle about within the 'lanterns' must never be eaten.

The Figs against the wall under the kitchen window have been ripe for some time now and it has been a good year for them. Fig trees need to be uncomfortable and cramped to fruit well, so their root-run should be restricted for best results, and they must always have a south- or west-facing wall. Figs are very unusual in that they have no visible flowers. These actually form and ripen their seeds in the complete darkness within the skin of the fruit.

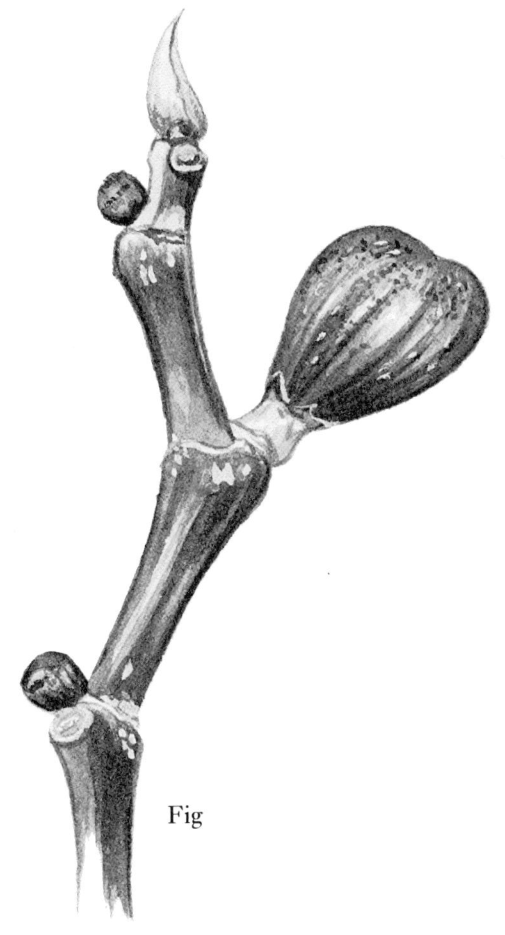

Fig

Common Oak

13 October

As always, the hips are worth waiting for. The most spectacular ones of the garden this year have been the dangling clusters of *R. rubrifolia*, because their subdued crimson glow contrasts so elegantly with the blue leaves of this charming rose. 'Nevada' has its off-years, but this year is a good one and the dark crimson hips are very fine. *R. moyesii* can almost be counted upon to provide its striking long bottle-shapes, and the hips of 'Cupid' are fat and orange and will glow all winter long. 'Frau Dagmar Hastrup' is a lovely rose who produces beautiful autumn colouration, particularly in a dry year. As this summer has, for once, been quite summery, the leaf-sprays are autumnally red and yellow, with the small dark jewels of the hips completing the harmony.

The year seems to culminate in a party-feeling at this time. The days are still warm, but the pace of growing has quite ceased, and most of the plants and trees have come to the end of their cycle. To celebrate this they put on the best that is in their wardrobes and wear it joyously for a few brief weeks – sometimes a few days only, as in the case of the *Gingko biloba* whose leaves turn to a clear butter-yellow, and almost before you can invite your friends to admire it, they are all blown away in the October gales.

That pleasant little relative of my *Cornus elegantissima*, *Cornus canadensis*, whose name has been changed to something much harder to spell, remember and pronounce, *Chamaepericlymenum canadensis*, is colouring nicely in the very dry corner under the Laburnum. This low-growing Cornus, never more than 6 inches (15.50cm) in height, will colonize steadily by means of its creeping underground rootstock. In June each leaf-rosette will produce a neat white 'flower' that lasts almost two months. In reality, the 'flower' consists of four enlarged white bracts surrounding the central group of tiny purplish flowers. Later there will be scarlet berries, and in October the leaves are quite spectacular, with colours that range through pink, crimson, maroon, green and black, all on one leaf-rosette. This plant needs an acid soil or woodland conditions to succeed, and a bank of it in full glory twice a year is well worth the inital trouble in getting the soil to its contentment. My garden has a pH factor of about 6, which is too neutral for this Cornus, so I have to bring in leaf-mould at least twice a year to keep it happy.

Glory Vine

17 October

The Virginia Creeper (*Parthenocissus quinquefolia*, syn *Vitis hederacea*) on the back wall opposite the kitchen window has been reddening daily through the last few weeks, and now it seems at its best. Most people plant this lovely creeper against their house walls where, if the house is of red brick, the green leaves of summer look very well; but come the autumn, and the intense brilliance of the crimson and scarlet leaves against the red brick is not a pleasing combination. I have seen Virginia Creeper planted to grow up through mature Silver Birches or Pines and *then* it is a glorious sight. A mature Pine tree with a crimson cloak of Virginia Creeper draped and dripping from its shoulders looks spectacular, and in a different way the more fragile delicacy of a Silver Birch is made even more interesting by these same scarlet leaves, because the Silver Birch turns yellow at this time of year and the two colours together have tremendous impact. Virginia Creeper will grow enormous with time, so if you have a bungalow, dig the creeper up and plant it elsewhere where it can spread itself or you will come back from a holiday one day to find that *Parthenocissus quinquefolia* has swallowed up your home.

Another creeper that acts in a slightly more restrained fashion is *Parthenocissus henryana*. This is a delicate-leaved self-clinging climber with dark leaves that have clearly marked veins and midribs in pink and white. In autumn, for a brief period of time, the dark green leaves turn brilliant crimson and the venation is even more clearly distinct at this time. This creeper likes a semi-shaded and sheltered situation, not being reliably hardy, so here it is planted against the west wall of the house where it has space to spread. The rose 'Morning Jewel' often gives us a spray or two of its bright cerise flowers at this time of year, and as the two are planted close together against the wall there is a last bright glow here before the creeper loses its brilliant leaves and the last of the rose petals fall. The *Vitis coignetiae* is living up to its name of 'Glory Vine' this year – how well it shows up against the sombre green of the vulgar *Leylandii* hedge.

19 October

The blaze of fire that is the Guelder Rose (*Viburnum opulus*) is well worth the space that it will eventually occupy – about 15 × 15 feet (456cm × 456cm). Hanging from the branches are the pendulous jelly-jewels that are its fruits; for some reason, the birds do not take them and they remain long after the wonderfully coloured leaves have fallen. This is the Viburnum having the flat corymbs of white blossom made up of large sterile 'flowers' (in reality, these are bracts) surrounding the small scented true flowers in the middle. *Viburnum opulus* demands no special care, and repays this lack most handsomely in the autumn with leaves that are green and yellow, yellow and orange, orange and

Virginia Creeper

scarlet, scarlet and crimson, crimson and tawny-brown. All at once as I am watching it, the bush seems to flicker with colour as the wind blows.

When choosing flowering shrubs and when space is at a premium, it is as well to choose shrubs or trees that oblige twice a year – with flowers in spring, harmony of colour in the autumn and sometimes with edible fruit as well, such as the flowering and fruiting crabs. *Amelanchier canadensis* has a positive froth of white blossom in the spring, and its leaves are brilliant crimson in the autumn. Azaleas have spring flowers and the leaves of deciduous varieties sometimes turn a universal bright and shining scarlet before they fall. *Cornus* 'Florida' has pink 'flowers' (another shrub whose bracts look like flowers), *Cornus* 'Kousa' has white ones, and both have wonderful autumnal colour. *Viburnum tomentosum mariesii* has tiers of white flowers in early summer and the whole bush turns to a dull and even crimson later in the year. Fothergillas have attractive fluffy white flowers in the spring, but it is for autumn colour that this bush is grown – the leaves turn to shades of yellow, orange, scarlet and dark red.

Guelder Rose

Chamaepericlymenum canadensis

Liquidambar styraciflua – the Sweet Gum – is a small tree with leaves of a perfect maple-shape that change to astonishing shades of orange, scarlet and crimson in a good autumn. Another shrub that has brilliant autumn colour is Enkianthus (there are three varieties), but this needs acid soil conditions. *Nyssa sylvatica* is a small tree from the Eastern United States that is equally spectacular, and though this does not actually require an acid soil, its situation must be quite free of lime. One could go on for pages about the subtleties – or the stridencies – of autumn colouration, but if the subject is interesting to you then a visit should be made to an arboretum or a good shrub and tree nursery during this time of year. The best times for colour fluctuate by a week or so either way each year, according to the weather of the preceding months, so it is worth finding out before the journey is made as to exactly when is the best time to make your visit.

In the hedgerows the Dogwood (another Cornus – *C. sanguinea*) is turning deep red, and as one goes along the country roads one can see patches of solid crimson in the hedges that indicate groups of Dogwood bushes. Some years these seem to shade from dark red to prussian-blue, and in other years they are a deep carmine.

22 October

This is a time of spider-webs silvered in dawn dew and early morning mist, and if I go down to the studio before breakfast, there are floating silken barriers across the path.

The tall bronze Fennel in the herb-bed is misted all over with tiny droplets, and at the top of each stem there is a sparkling jewel, captured in the cupped wheel of the green flower-stalks. In the thin gold October sunlight they look like chalices of crystal, and in an hour they will be gone.

On the tree that overhangs the gate into the paddock the apples are ripe, and as there was wind in the night, some of the fruit has fallen and lies broken on the stones of the path, making an easy autumn banquet for the late butterflies. Some of these apples were rotten before they fell, and this more matured cider-mash is much appreciated. This afternoon I saw a Comma, wings together, listing slowly sideways as he sipped at the potent juices, quite heedless of the wheel-barrow passing to and fro less than nine inches away. I was cutting and clearing the exuberant growth of one of the summer borders, and was making many journeys to the compost-heap in the field. The Comma ignored me, so far gone was he in liquor. But the Red Admiral butterflies (or 'Red Admirables' as they used to be called) seem to favour the apples from the trees on the lower lawn, whose fruit ripens early in the autumn; the Red Admirables share my preference for it but they lack moderation. They will gorge and gorge until they, too, fall over sideways, and it is possible to pick them up gently and place them on a branch out of harm's way. Their feet have tiny claws and, even in this state of complete inebriation, it is quite possible to 'hook' them on to the rough tree-bark to recover.

The robin is back in the garden again; he 'disappears' during the summer months during his moult. Now that he has returned, his quick, flicking flight and bright vest are always in the corner of my field of vision as I go about the garden, autumn-tidying. He has an afternoon bath quite regularly at four o'clock in the shallow puddle of rainwater that lies in the fossil footprint. With the robin is his friend the wren, creeping in and out of the fern-fronds that grow at the base of this great stone. The robin dips and splashes and scoops the water and leaves all over himself – what bright eyes he has, and how disreputable he looks after his bath! He flies off to preen and sort out his feathers, the wren waits for a moment and then flies after him to land on the same branch of the Weigela bush. I watch, and there is no squabbling, as there would be with sparrows or starlings. The robin and the wren fly together about the garden, and it is easy to see why, in medieval times, the wren was called the robin's wife. In those days, the robin was thought to bring bad luck and domestic disaster if he flew in through an open door or window. Now he has been Christmas-carded into respectability.

I have come to the conclusion that my garden is full of wilful and obstinate plants who know their own requirements best. For example, the *Schizostylis coccinea* shouldn't even be there! This delicate and tender plant comes from South Africa, with rushy leaves and exquisite pink or red starry flowers in late autumn. They seemed quite happy at the end of the rockery, but I felt that they were not getting enough sun. They were lifted and placed in one of the best south-facing positions in the garden, at the base of the low boundary wall. After two years they had disappeared, but in the original patch of ground near the rockery the leaves had returned last year, then buds appeared and the stems are once more beautiful with fragile pink stars. There seems to be a moral here somewhere, as there is all the time in an old garden.

Dogwood

28 October

A little bit of autumn colour goes a long way, and one has to visualize where the brightness should be in the garden. This is where the conifers come in – as a background foil to the sudden autumn conflagration, and it is better to do as much of the planning as possible on paper because one does not then have to wait a whole season to rectify the errors or to make the improvements.

There has been much rain for the last ten days, and in the clear intervals between the showers and downpours it has been pleasant to take a walk in the dripping woods before all the leaves are gone from the trees. I needed the leaves of the Sweet Chestnut (*Castanea sativa*) for an illustration, and I wanted them at the precise moment when some of the leaves on the tree would be bright yellow, some tawny-gold, some light brown and some still green. This was asking a lot, but I knew that if I walked for long enough and for far enough I should both fill my pockets with Chestnuts and find what I sought, and meanwhile enjoy the tranquillity of the trees.

Hips of Rose Cupid

Some of the Chestnut trees were wholly yellow – these were the younger, smaller ones – but others in shadier situations were still all-green. Others had achieved a fine compromise with all the colours together on one branch, and it was one of these that I hoped to capture. The Chestnuts themselves had fallen out of their prickly armour and were lying on the ground, ready for all to gather up; I wished that I had brought a basket, so many were there because of the wind and the rain of the preceding weeks. Compromising with a Dick-Whittington-like arrangement of stick and scarf, I soon had it full. How sad it is these days: the harvest of woodland and hedgerow is still there for all, but less and less folk seem to avail themselves of it. But I met some nutting boys, complete with muddy dog, sticks and bags – at least *this genus* of homo sapiens has not changed much. Sweet Chestnuts are not indigenous to Britain but were introduced long ago by the Romans, thereafter spreading all over the British Isles.

Docks are detestable, and are even disliked by donkeys who will consume *almost* anything and by goats who will eat what a donkey leaves. If one has a small paddock with a normal growth of Docks in it, any livestock imported into it to keep the grass down will carefully eat all round the Docks, leaving them standing up stark and tall to scatter the next generation of seeds. In the autumn when the grass has either been eaten or has been beaten down by the rains, the docks are still there, just as stiff and upright, though now they have turned to a deep rust-brown and are the more visible because of it. Docks have no censer mechanism, nor have they winged seed, hooks or any means of propulsion – but nothing proliferates like a Dock.

A tiny plant might appear in the rock-garden in the spring, and because it is so tiny it goes unnoticed except by its immediate neighbour, who will gradually be crowded against the rocky sides of its home by the quickly fattening root and the spreading lower leaves of the villain Dock. By midsummer, the Dock will have smothered the more sensitive soul of the rock-plant and will then have the crevice all to itself. This is, of course, if you do not notice it, but even if you do, and cut off its head, as the Red Queen said to Alice, you have to remember to keep doing it and a Dock seems to be able to survive constant beheading better than any other plant I know.

I have a treasured rarity in the greenhouse that is in a very delicate state of health and which is being nursed slowly back to strength and vitality. A Dock seed got into the pot by some means and, though scissored off every time it grows a new leaf, it has not given up the fight to survive yet. I do not dare disturb the roots of the rightful occupant, as it is only just beginning to put forth the first shy new leaves. So I keep beheading the Dock, but it seems to be getting larger and larger. There are many varieties of Dock but they all have strong kinships to each other and are difficult to tell apart.

1 November

One of the more astonishing colours of autumn is seen in the squid-blue tones of some varieties of Hydrangea, usually the Hortensia group. One has seen their fading blue flowers now for many months and because of their familiarity they have become, if not invisible, at least so taken for granted that one walks past them without noticing the subtle changes in their colouration. These can be almost any shade from bronze-green through all the various shades of pink and very deep crimson to the more sinister vegetable colours of violet and indigo. My Hydrangea 'Blue Bonnet' is changing most interestingly and though the leaves are still the usual light apple-green, they are beginning to shade through yellow and rose-pink to a bright violet – exactly the colour of love-letter ink. The flowers were the same shade of purple last week, edged with cerise, and now they are prussian-blue and turquoise.

Parrotia persica

Later still when the frosts come the flowers will change to a modest brown. The mop-heads of Hydrangeas should be left on the plant for protection, and in any case they make the garden look a little more 'clothed' during this time of few flowers. The *Parrotia persica* has put on its autumn ball-gown of shocking pink, salmon, scarlet and yellow. All the leaves are different and some of them still have green veins, or even, for contrast, green edges. This is a shrub that sits quietly by during spring and summer, with absolutely nothing to say for itself. It has very small and inconspicuous flowers in late spring, but Cinderella really goes to the ball in the autumn when this member of the Hazel family lives up to its very appropriate name. Every year it has a different colour-tone, and I suppose much depends on the weather, the amount of rain during the season, the severity of the first frosts, the temperature of the soil and the position of the shrub in the garden. I have seen some Parrotias that change only to tones of sombre yellow, but this one seems to have brushed against the palette of an impressionist painter, so bright are its colours.

The Nerines are still flowering – what a joy these plants are at this dark time of short days and inclement, if not positively vicious weather. Their rosy pinkness always seems quite unbelievable at this season, just as Crown Imperials seem equally unbelievable in a frozen English garden in March.

4 November

Winter is here. There was a sharp frost in the night, and one is so used to walking over the yielding surface of the lawn that walking over frozen ground that is curiously bumpier than usual comes as a surprise as well as a jolt to the spine. The whole garden is assuming tones of yellow now, even the great Weigela is a huge and perfect dome of this colour. But very soon there will be no leaves at all.

8 November

Dangling apples on the two trees by the field gate reminded me that they should all have been picked three weeks ago. These are eating apples whose name is unknown, and each year another good intention is to send some to Wisley to find out what they are. I know that giving them a name at last will make them all taste even better, except the strange red-skinned one in the field which doesn't seem good for anything at all.

By the pond the fluffy and long-lasting flowers of the aromatic Water-mint (*Mentha aquatica*), the sky-coloured Water Forget-me-not (*Myosotis scorpioides*), the dull red of Water Avens (*Geum rivale*), the bright sun-gold of Kingcups (*Caltha palustris*), the pale lilac of March Violet (*Viola palustris*), the furry brown bulrushes of *Typha angustifolia*, the airy white lightness of Water Plantain

Chrysanthemum 'Balcombe Perfection'

(*Alisma plantago-aquatica*), the bright yellow of *Iris pseudacorus* and the striking pink beauty of the Flowering Rush (*Butomus umbellatus*) all live and multiply. With the Monkey flower (*Mimulus luteus*) and the two or three Water-lilies that crowd the middle of the pond, there is plenty of interest except just after Boxing Day when all is neat and tidy and just a little bit too clinical.

I have some Double Kingcups which I shall give away, because, on the whole, I do not care for double flowers. Having said this I cannot recommend too highly the gentle-coloured lilac flowers of the double-flowered Lady's Smock (*Cardamine pratensis flore pleno*) that spreads slowly and prettily all along the edges of the paths hereabouts. The reference books say that double flowers have no seeds (this is why I dislike them), yet this little plant pops up as individual 'seedlings' all over the nearby borders. It is quite charming and very floriferous in spring, producing dozens of lilac-flowered stems that grow very closely together, so that the clumps and mats of the plant are a solid mass of this rather uncommon spring colour.

Common Polypody

Nerine

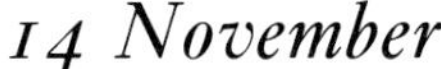

14 November

I am so glad that ferns are coming back into fickle fashion, and have always loved them in any case. There are eight varieties in the garden and each year I add a new one to the collection. They are so graceful (in most cases) and so very *green*, and are quite invaluable in town gardens, revelling as they do in the extra warmth that a city generates and being quite content in the very difficult corners of small town gardens where there is very little sun or often none at all. They will even tolerate poor, sad soil, though in these conditions they will merely do their duty and not their best. The more delicate and 'special' varieties will need proper conditions, but the strong wild ferns will grow almost as greenly as they would in their natural habitats. As well as the wavy satin ribbons of the Hart's-Tongue Fern (*Asplenium scolopendrium*) there is the even more common Polypody (*Polypodium vulgare*), which is quite happy to grow almost anywhere, tolerating very dry situations as widely separated in nature as a fork in the trunk of a patriarchal oak and the hedge bottom that grows at its feet, where most of the other vegetation has longer and stronger roots.

The Male Fern (*Dryopteris felix-mas*) is a very typical and characteristic fern that looks like a frozen green fountain throughout the summer beside the path. The clumps are gradually increasing in size and I must split them up during their dormant period, which will be very soon now. One of the treasures of the garden is *Polystichium setiferum densum*, which is evergreen even in the hardest of winters. This grows beside the path, next to the *Phormium tenax*, and both are much admired by the visitors. The *setiferum* came to me as a single frond, and it is relatively easy to grow, unlike most other ferns. It produces bulbils along the centre rib of the frond that can be snipped into as many sections as there are bulbils; each one should be laid carefully on a bed of moist compost and covered lightly with more of the same. The seed-box that contains all these infant ferns should be left outside in a shady place and not allowed to dry out; the tiny ferns will begin to sprout from the bulbils within a few weeks. I did two seedboxes full in August and placed them under the shelter of the wide Phormium leaves, where even the rain is channelled away. To date, at least ten tiny ferns have appeared and I am sure that there will be more in due course.

Maidenhair fern (*Adiantum capillus veneris*) sometimes dies out altogether here, because it prefers a much wetter situation than I can provide for it, though this will be remedied this winter. At the edge of one of the waterfalls in the rockery we deliberately built in a 'leak' in order to encourage the then very tiny Dryopteris which was so delighted with its good fortune that it has grown enormous and now shades everything at that end of the rockery. This winter we will get it all out and plant in its place a Maidenhair, which will also love the waterfall beside it and the trickle of water across its feet.

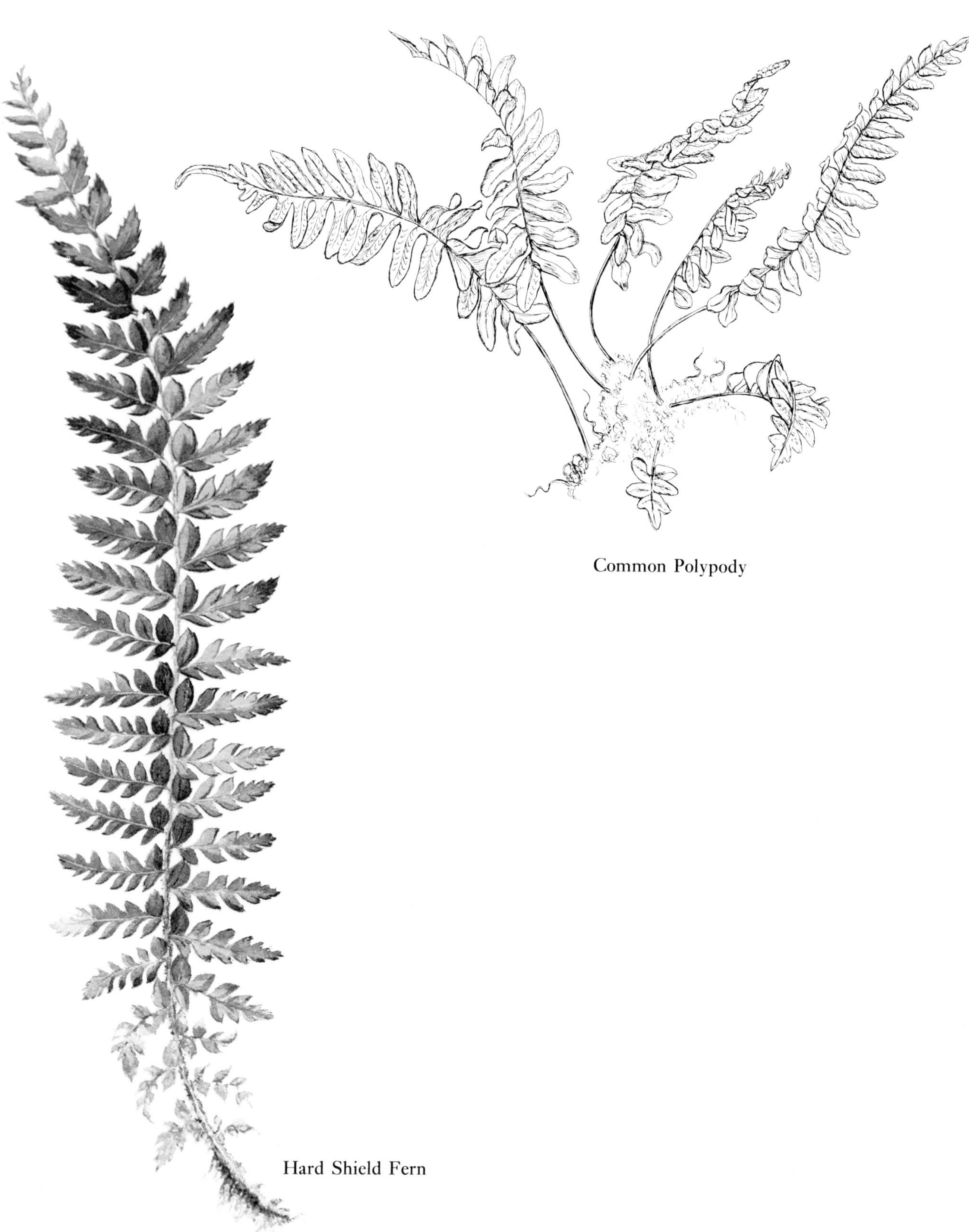

Common Polypody

Hard Shield Fern

Hydrangea

The Hard Shield Fern (*Polystichium aculeatum*) is a very handsome glossy green fern that likes a lime-rich soil and a shady place to live. The Broad Buckler Fern (*Dryopteris dilatata*) is another graceful and strong-growing wild fern that looks particularly at home growing at the base of the apple tree on the lower lawn. The Ostrich-Feather Fern (*Matteuccia struthiopteris*) is the most beautiful of them all and exactly resembles its name, looking like a light-green plume of Prince of Wales feathers. There are two more 'mystery' ferns that live outside in pots during the summer, but these have to go back into the safety of the greenhouse for the winter, and as they were gifts I do not know their names. They do not resemble any of our native ferns, so must be tender exotics from some steamy jungle – or so I like to think.

The garden's free-draining soil is very good for almost everything else but not for the fern family, and I cosset them with sackfuls of leafmould and much extra watering in dry summers. I love the fascination of the crisp golden-brown uncurling fronds in the spring, so soon to change to the most delightful shade of fresh, bright green which in turn sobers down in later summer. The gracefulness of fern-fronds along any shady path, or growing against the bole of a tree or at the base of a flight of steps, is something that needs to be seen to be remembered again from those days of childhood, when we saw all these things so often but never stopped to think much about them.

Many ferns remain green in winter, so are of considerable garden value. They are difficult to propagate, having a totally different method of reproduction from flowers – because they have no flowers, though that most noble member of the family, the Royal Fern (*Osmunda regalis*), has fertile brown fronds growing in the centre of the clump resembling flower-heads.

15 November

The very popular *Cotoneaster horizontalis* is a mass of scarlet berries on the wall by the front gate. This shrub is seen so often under bay windows for the very good reason that it seldom grows more than three feet high. It is a very good-tempered plant that can be grown almost anywhere, and one which will clothe a north-facing wall with bee-crowded flowers in spring and brief brilliant foliage in autumn, with exactly-matching berries that last until the following year unless the winter is a very hard one. In which case the sparrows and other birds of the garden will squabble over the berries for several days, and will strip the flat, herring-boned branches bare. During a mild winter when there is plenty of other food about, the berries will stay until early spring.

This is an excellent shrub for covering those inconvenient drain-covers that thoughtless builders leave in conspicuous places on the lawn. The bush can be planted to one side of the cover, and will obligingly mound itself over it, and can be helped a little if necessary with the secateurs. In three years you will never remember that you had such a thing as a drain-cover.

16 November

The sun is shining and the temperature is a mild 60°F, so I have abandoned the drawing-board for the day, leaving my feelings of guilt and contrition neatly stacked beside the sharpened pencils. Out in the garden it is difficult to know where to begin, so on the principle of tidying up where it is untidiest I went round with the sharpest pair of shears and collected four barrowloads in half an hour.

There is a fine clump of bronze Chrysanthemums – *C.* 'Balcombe Perfection' – that began life as a rather special pot-plant which eventually readjusted itself to the reality of life in a garden. The flowers have large heavy heads and need

Bracken

careful staking, otherwise they will be overcome by the wet. I do not recommend this particular variety for the garden, for there are many other hardy types that will not need the cosseting that this one has enjoyed. After the flowers are over in late autumn, Chrysanthemum plants should always be cut down to ground level in December.

I like this month, because when cutting down the frost-blackened stems of those near relatives of the Chrysanthemum, the Michaelmas Daisies, one knows that they will be back to greet the world again in late spring, which is only just the other side of Christmas.

Path-sweeping today was a very necessary job because wet leaves lying on a path can be very hazardous. Wet leaves lying on the lawn do no good either, because if they lie there in drifts to rot, the grass beneath will suffer. For lawns the old-fashioned besom or birch broom is excellent because it has a whisking action that a broom does not have. Leaf-sweeping should only be done on a windless day, and when the heaps of leaves are either swept or raked together, then one uses the old-fashioned method of two thin flat boards to gather them up into the barrow. I have a wire-netting bin in the field reserved solely for leaves, and it is always surprising to see how small a quantity of leaf-compost eventually results from a lawnful of leaves.

Viburnum bodnantense Dawn

Iris foetidissima

20 November

The buds are forming on the Wintersweet (*Chimonanthus praecox*) against the east wall, but that other sweet-scented shrub *Viburnum bodnantense* 'Dawn' is in full bloom and sending out little eddies of perfume. This shrub needs a sunny and sheltered position, and though this particular Viburnum is rather inconspicuous in summer and does not colour very excitingly in autumn, in the dark days of November and December the pink flowers appear in terminal clusters all along the bare branches and they last very well in water.

There is another plant that is flowering away, quite unabashed by the appalling weather of the last few weeks; this is *Colletia armata*, which books assure me 'can grow to 10 feet' (3m). This shrub has small and inconspicuous bell-shaped pink flowers and is only remarkable for the vicious spininess of all its parts; it out-Gorses Gorse any time because the spikes are thicker and firmer. I planted it as a tiny cutting near the fossil footprint, when this part of the garden had plenty of space, but it is now four feet (1.2m) high and its presence here is going to cause this part of the path to become a prickly cul-de-sac instead of a scaled-down ravine.

Thinking and planning (and planting accordingly) at this time of year is worth any amount of hasty planting from container-pots in late spring, because the plants will have the benefit of the slowly warming soil in their new environment. The exceptions are the grey- and silver-leaved herbaceous things which often vanish soggily for ever if the winter is more than usually wet. I know that panes of glass propped on wire legs are not very sightly, but they do protect the Christmas Roses from mud-splashes, the Sempervivums from too much wet and the 'silvers' from too much rain, which they hate.

28 November

The Periwinkles (*Vinca major* and *V. major* 'variegata') have begun their winter flowering. These scorned and despised cottage garden flowers are very welcome here at this and any other time of the year because they flower undismayed by all the unpleasantness of the weather. The variegated-leaved one is trying to climb into the lower branches of the *Prunus pissardii* above it, while the evergreen shape of the Escallonia provides a perfect background for its light-coloured cream and green leaves.

Evergreens (a term that always reminds me of school spinach) come into their own at this time of year, making blocks of green solidity among all the bare twigs and branches. *Eleagnus pungens* 'maculata' grows near the Escallonia, and its shiny yellow leaves, narrowly bordered in dark green, are a delight to see throughout the winter. *Aucuba japonica* 'maculata' will grow absolutely anywhere, and its light green spotted leaves will brighten up a shady corner very

Apples on the path

Common Ivy

Sloe

effectively. Of course, the *Garrya elliptica* is evergreen and has very attractive waved leaves, though these are often scorched and blackened by the frosts. All varieties of Mahonia are handsomely evergreen, and the large serrated leaves in their huge rosettes are particularly valuable in the winter garden. Some Viburnums are evergreen, such as *V. davidii*, and that useful seaside plant *Griselinia littoralis* is a particularly pleasing shade of pale apple green throughout the year, though it has no flowers to speak of. When it does bloom the flowers are insignificant and appear in spring. It is dioecious.

In the lawn the three most vigorous weeds are doing well and are greener and more vigorous than the tired grass. I mean by this the Daisies, Dandelions and Plantains, and though I love 'lawn-Daisies' I will have to do something about them this year because parts of the lawn are more Daisy than grass. But when it comes to Plantains there is no room for sentiment. Plantains have no charm for me at all, because their flat plates of leaves will grow ever larger, killing all the grass thus shaded. So, today I dug them all up, leaving great pocks and holes which had to be filled with soil. This job would have been better attended by success in the spring, because then I could have sown grass-seed in the new soil, but in the spring I am quite sure that I will be busy once more at the drawing board and once more the Plantains will be spared.

There are two types of Plantain, but the one that plagues gardeners with pretensions to good lawns is *Plantago major* – the Greater Plantain. This has long green pokers as flowers, whereas the Ribwort Plantain (*Plantago lanceolata*) has narrower leaves and shorter, darker flower-spikes. There are many stories about the Plantain and one of them is that the Red Indians of North America called the plant 'White Man's Foot' because it was found wherever the early settler had passed. Plantains do have their uses, and were formerly used as wound herbs, that is, they were washed, bruised to a pulp and applied in the form of a poultice to wounds. The leaves can still be used today in the same manner for insect bites and wasp and bee stings, though the plants used must be taken from a garden unpolluted by chemicals. So I shall leave a few plantains in case the bees take against me.

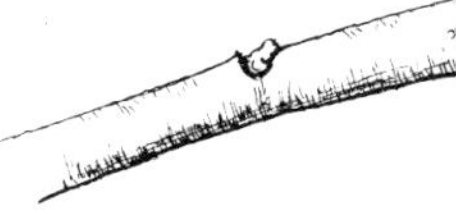

The last apple

December

5 December

The Winter Jasmine (*Jasminum nudiflorum*) is always such a joy, with its showers of starry yellow flowers on the bare brushy branches. This is another amiable shrub that will grow almost anywhere, but if it is planted where it will receive at least half a day's sun it will reward you during the darkest days of winter with what sometimes seems almost like a firework display of flowers. Winter Jasmine needs a little support for its scandent habit, and without this it will bend over and lie along the ground, which will certainly not show off the flowers to their best advantage.

Frost will put paid to the current crop of bloom, but the Jasmine's flowering season is long – from November until April – so as soon as the winter temperature improves, a new flush of flowers will greet it. The branches can be picked for the vases when in bud, and the flowers will then open in water. In late spring when the flowers have gone, this Jasmine should be cut back and the oldest and woodiest stems should be removed to make way for the new growths.

The variegated Holly 'Silver Queen' at the back of the cottage has grown large enough to give up some of its branches to help with the Christmas decorations. I was warned by the greengrocer that Holly was in short supply this year, though I cannot think why, as all the bushes and trees in the hedges have been bright with berries for weeks. I must beg a few green Holly boughs from my friend with the leaf-mould because Christmas isn't Christmas without the dark shine of Holly leaves, though Cotoneaster and Pyracantha berries can be artfully intermixed when the Holly's own berries are in short supply to present the traditional mix of red and green.

Holly

Ivy (*Hedera helix*) can be used as well, though this plant was never used in medieval times to deck the churches because fairies and elves were included among the guests at Christmastide. This was the only time in the year when mankind was safe from their mischief, the spirits having no powers to harm at Christmas. Branches of Ivy were hung in outer porches, halls and passages to accommodate the little people, who were able to cling to the smooth leaves. These decorations were put up on Christmas Eve and taken down on Candlemas Eve (1 February) and it was considered very unlucky to bring the Ivy further into the houses than the outer halls and passages.

There is always an uncomfortable feeling of bad luck when Ivy is used in the house at these times and this is a folk-memory from times gone by. The Holly and the Ivy had more power at this time of the year to subdue evil spirits and in Scotland Ivy was used as an amulet or talisman to protect the kine, being hung over the door of the cow-byre. Ivy was used again on May-day Eve, which was a dangerous time to be abroad. Ivies come into their own in a garden in winter when all the summer leaves have flown away in the autumn gales.

When I counted the varieties of Ivy in the garden they numbered seven, which rather surprised me as I had not thought there were as many. Growing slowly back along the fence is the beautiful (and slightly tender) *Hedera helix canariensis 'variegata'* 'Gloire de Marengo', which is among the handsomest of them all and which is probably the best known. When we first came here I rather absent-mindedly took some cuttings and they all grew. Most of them

Common Ivy

I gave away, but now the house is almost girdled with 'Gloire de Marengo' because one of the cuttings was planted against the back yard wall and it liked it so much that it grew into a stout pillar of beautiful leaves that mounted the wall and is now scrambling about along the top and falling down on the other side in a river of variegated leaves, whose colours of green, grey and cream are often flushed with pink during the winter months.

Another 'Gloire de Marengo' cutting was planted at the end of the yard nearest the street, and this has wound itself prettily through the old iron fence in front of the cottage, where nothing will grow because of the shade and the pollution from the road. Yet another was planted at the other front corner of the cottage, and these two will soon meet and clasp hands. I think that this would have happened some time ago but for the Russian Vine (*Polygonatum baldschuanicum*), whose presence has a very inhibiting effect on the Ivy which puts on a spurt of growing in late winter and early spring to compensate for being smothered throughout the summer. Many people scorn Russian Vine, as they scorn Marigolds, Love-in-a-Mist, Aubrieta, Buddleia and Scarlet Pelargoniums, probably because these need little attention or special care. Russian Vine is certainly the quickest cover-up that can be planted, and its long arms can achieve 40 feet (12m) in a single season.

Hedera helix canariensis 'variegata' Gloire de Marengo

Winter Jasmine

Hedera helix 'Sagittaefolia' lives up to its name, having delicate arrow-shaped leaves, and was planted at the other side of the mound of rocks by the fossil footprint, where it is doing its best to colonize the whole bed. I shall be firm with it in the spring, and shall take hundreds of cuttings – I cannot bear to cast anything as attractive as this into the compost-heap, where in any case it would take many months to rot down. *Hedera helix* 'Goldheart' is well known and is a slow-growing small-leaved Ivy with very attractive green-edged yellow leaves. It does not strike very easily from cuttings, and the percentage of success is less than a third, but as there is plenty and to spare of 'Goldheart' on top of the rockery, I shall try again next year.

Hedera helix 'Conglomerata' lives up to its name and is a queer upstanding thing that does not behave as other Ivies do. It needs no support and grows in a rigid and free-standing way, with short, stiff stems thickly clothed with small dark green leaves. It should be planted in a rockery or at the edge of a path where it can be easily seen. Under the larder window *Hedera helix* 'Green Ripple' is growing strongly now after a slow start. This Ivy has medium-sized green leaves with a characteristic shape and clearly marked veins. It is quite happy here and is sending self-clinging branches upwards to cover the window, and these look very attractive against the light wall. I am quite happy that the larder window should be covered in this way because in mid-summer the sun comes in during the late afternoon and the cool green shade of the Ivy leaves will be most effective as a permanent and evergreen sun-blind.

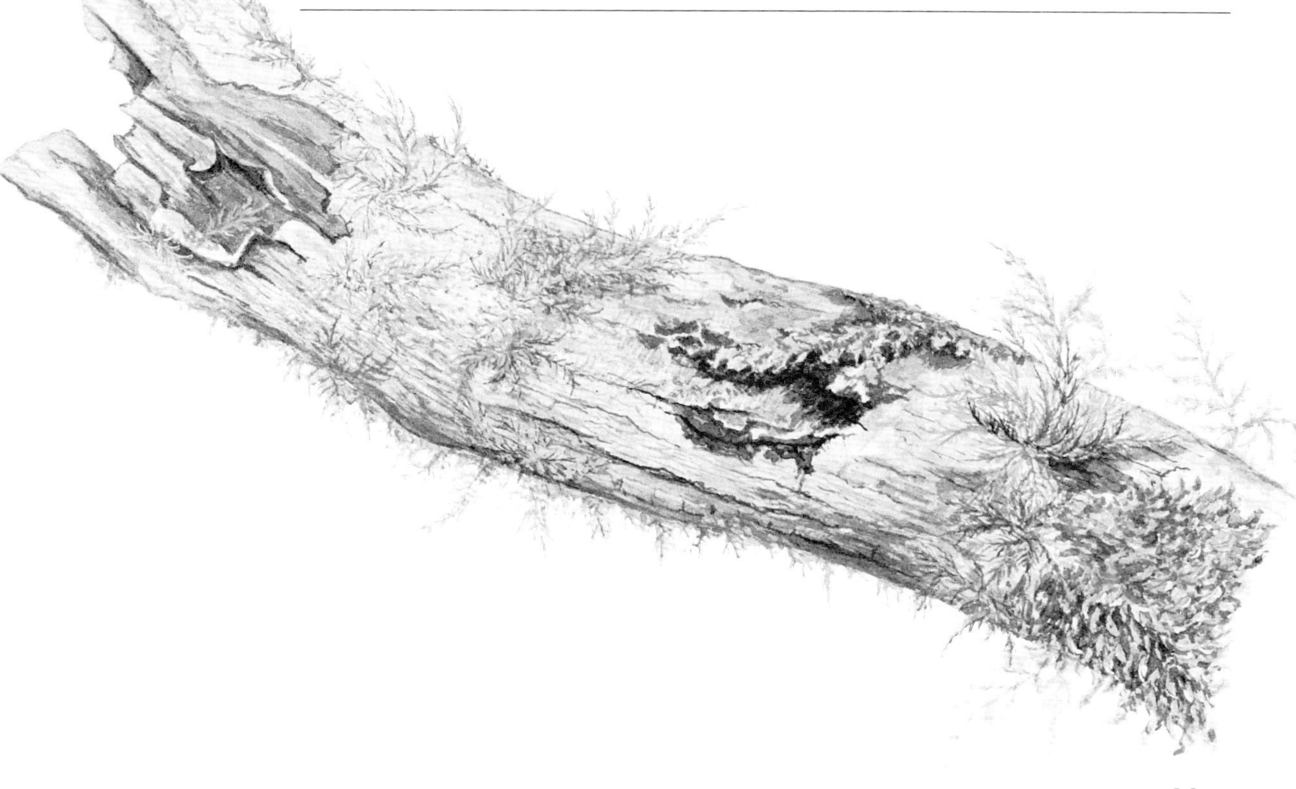

Moss

Hedera helix 'Silver Queen' syn 'Marginata' climbs in a busy spiral round and about one of the porch pillars. This is another pretty little small-leaved ivy whose leaves are variegated green and cream with pink edges to them in winter. It was given to me as an indoor pot-plant, but I felt that it would be happier outside and it has a very sheltered situation here. One of the successful cuttings of 'Goldheart' climbs more slowly up and round the other post, but it is not so vigorous and, in any case, 'Silver Queen' has had two years start. Under the studio windows, and desperately needing to be moved because of the Bamboo above it that will most surely choke it to death next year, is another larger-leaved Ivy, *Hedera helix dentata* 'Aurea', which has large yellow variegations, otherwise being very similar to 'Gloire de Marengo'. I will take some 'insurance' cuttings in the spring before I attempt to move this one – just in case.

And of course, creeping about at the base of all the old walls in the garden is our very common native species *Hedera helix*, itself never far from man's habitation.

12 December

It was a bright blue sort of day today, and as I had had no interruptions I finished a painting in record time and felt that I had earned an outing. Combining pleasure with philanthropy and academic interest I visited a favourite but overgrown nursery a few miles away where all manner of strange shrubs and trees peer at the visitor through a haze of brambles, and where there is a marvellous sense of tranquillity and peace. I have often gone there just to walk round and be quite alone when, as happens in all our lives, it is absolutely essential for sanity's sake to go away to somewhere quiet.

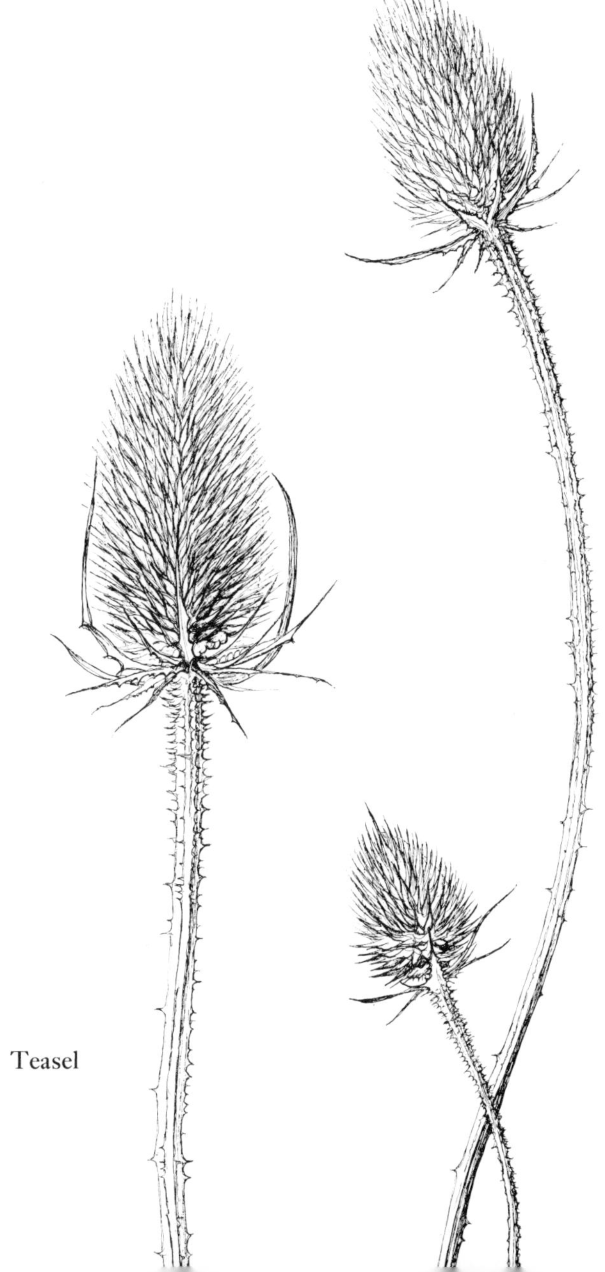

Teasel

As I walked about quite briskly, because the bright blue day was proving seasonally chilly, an interesting-looking tree in a far corner caught my eye. Its scarlet droplets, seen against the cold cobalt sky, turned out to be the fruits of a full-grown *Sorbus Zahlbruckneri*, which is a cousin of our native *Sorbus aucuparia* – the Rowan or Mountain Ash. *S. Zahlbruckneri* turns a fine yellow in autumn, and the little jewelled clusters of its fruits remain on the tree for several months, unless the winter is a hard one for the birds. An interesting nearby tree was the Snowdrop tree (*Halesia carolina*), which has bell-shaped white flowers in May. Now it is bare of leaves, but from its branches hung bunched clusters of dangling seed-pods intricately four-sided.

Scots Pine

Christmas Rose

Another tree that has clusters of pods is the Judas tree (*Cercis siliquastrum*), which is clothed along its branches in spring with bunches of pink pea-flowers that later turn to long, dangling pods. In maturity the tree can grow very large, but this will take many years. In a far corner, I saw a flash of ultramarine blue: this was *Viburnum davidii*, a dioecious evergreen shrub that produces corymbs of creamy-pink flowers. When male and female shrubs are planted together the resulting blue berries that last all through autumn and well into this month (provided they are sheltered from frosts) are really worth having because they are as eyecatching as sapphire jewellery. The flowers on both male and female bushes are so similar as to be indistinguishable except through a lens, and though two or more shrubs take up quite a space, they are very handsome throughout the year with their large, dark, deeply-veined leaves. The flowers are very similar to those of Laurustinus (*Viburnum tinus*) to which it is of course related.

Visiting a friend's garden on the way home from the nursery in order to present him (a little prematurely) with his Christmas present, I noticed that his Rosemary (*Rosmarinus officinalis*) was absolutely covered in flowers. Surely this must be a record for either exceptional lateness, or conversely, exceptional earliness.

21 December, 7.30 am

When I awake the birds are singing, except on those days when the weather is icy. This is always something of a surprise in winter, but it is nevertheless a delightful way in which to be woken, though it is nothing like as vociferous as the dawn chorus of a summer's day.

As I came up from the studio yesterday I noticed the first feint speckling of the Celandine leaves beneath the Weigela. Spring will soon be here and the garden is nothing like tidy enough to welcome it.

25 December

A mild and sunny day. For once the Christmas Roses (*Helleborus niger*) are the better through having been protected by a sheet of glass from the worst of the recent rains. The Holly trees in the district have plenty of berries (despite the greengrocer) and I know of an old apple tree with Mistletoe (*Viscum album*).

The jolly scarlet flowers of Poinsettias are now associated with Christmas, and I remember drawing them some years ago. The Poinsettia is more properly called *Euphorbia pulcherrima* and its brilliant scarlet (or pink, or white) 'flowers' are in reality bracts. The true flowers are small, yellow and inconspicuous in the centre of the inflorescence, and the 'petals', when seen as a drawing which of course has no colour, look exactly like the leaves with very similar venation. If someone has kindly given you a fine Poinsettia for a present, it has very definite dislikes and one of these is draughts. It likes humidity, a constant temperature of 55°F (13°C), and good light, and can be given a weak liquid feed almost as soon as you have unwrapped the pretty paper.

After the festive season is over it may tell you how unhappy it is by shedding its leaves, once by one, and there may be nothing much that you can do unless you have a heated greenhouse whose humidity-level will be more to its liking than a position in the centre of the dining-room table. Cut the stems down as soon as the flowers are over, and keep the soil just moist. Put the plant under the staging while the new leaves are coming. It does not like intense heat, and a temperature of over 64°F (18°C) will make it unhappy; and it can be stood outside in a shady place, once the weather is settled. It will need feeding every fortnight and regular watering from June until September. From this it will be seen that Poinsettias are pernickety and it will take about three years for them to learn to trust you. They are usually increased by cutting in the spring (use the pieces of shortened-back stem) and these should be dipped in powdered charcoal to arrest the flow of latex which all Euphorbias have. The cuttings should be placed in a mix of half and half peat and sand in a propagator set at a temperature of 64–70°F (18–21°C). When they have rooted and outgrown their first pots they can be potted on and will then need feeding, which should be given at fortnightly intervals.

30 December

These few days between Christmas and the New Year are very useful in the garden if the weather is suited to the work. Heavy rains or hard frost will put a full stop to productive activity, but these few and unexpectedly benevolent days in the no-man's land of time at the year's ending are good for the garden and the soul.

The rock-garden surrounding all the little pools looks neglected now. Almost half of it has been colonized by Galeobdolon or Yellow Archangel, whose proper name is *Lamiastrum galeobdolon* 'Variegatum'. This is an excellent ground-cover plant that can be easily controlled. It has pleasing silver-splashed leaves that show up well in the dusk, and in spring spires of pleasant yellow 'Deadnettle' flowers rise up through the tangle of leaves and stems. The plant sends out very long stoloniferous growths that root, if conditions are favourable, at each node. Each new rooting produces a new plant, but the stems that helped it are still there, joining all the new plants and making a foot-tangling network that covers the ground.

Cypress

Galeobdolon will grow almost anywhere, and looks fresh and vital throughout the year. Mature leaves are often green and black, with very distinctive silver splashes. I like this plant because of its willingness to clothe the dry ground beneath trees and bushes, but it does need sorting out about twice a year. After I had set about it with the shears, two or three small and slow-growing conifers must have taken the first breath of unconstricted air since the spring. One such is *Sequoia sempervirens adpressa*, which has interesting white-tipped shoots that look as though they have been dipped in whitewash. Near it is the truly dwarf *Chamaecyparis obtusa* 'Nana' that still looks almost Japanese in its smallness, and I am most grateful to the truthful nurseryman who sold it to me as being 'very dwarf and likely to stay so for many years'. This has upright green fans of leaves that look almost fossilized in their rigidity.

There is a jolly little collection of Houseleeks (*Sempervivum*) that are beginning to spread over the edges of the nearby rocks. Again, these are very undemanding plants that have such an interesting form, and an established colony of them is a fine sight. One should collect half a dozen or so with very different colouration and once they have settled in, all they want is to be left alone. They will produce infant plants from beneath themselves, and these will quickly increase in size, likewise producing children. One has to give them a little help from time to time, because the centre part of the group can get very congested, with fat little rosettes trying to find a foothold to grow in and being quite unable to because of the overcrowding. It is a bit like a seagull colony, and one has to thin out the middle a little and start the babies growing elsewhere. Birds frequently scratch them up for some reason, and I had to protect my collection with wire netting when they were small, because once out of the ground they dry up and die after a few days, though when they are growing they can exist in the driest of conditions – such as an old slate or tiled roof – as long as they are properly anchored down with their roots tucked into a crack.

Tiarella collina softens the path's edge with its pleasant year-round cushions of leaves and, in summer, the delicate greenish flowers. It is rather like *Heuchera* 'Greenfinch', whose leaves are evergreen and whose flowers are a fragile-looking froth of creamy-green. I have planted some seeds of the more ordinary *Heuchera sanguinea* which will take about two years to come to flowering size, but once they start they are most attractive, and will light up a shady path with their sparkling coral-coloured flowers. Heucheras have a way of growing right out of the soil, and in the autumn they have to be settled back in again, which means digging them up and re-planting them. During the summer this would upset them and prevent flowering, so one compromises by building up a mound of soil beneath the plant on which it can sit for the rest of the season. They are rather short-lived perennials, so I usually sow seeds every two years to keep a succession of good plants going.

Mistletoe

Euphorbia cyparissias grows here, its delicately soft blue-green leaves contrasting very pleasingly with a big rock just behind it. This is a low-growing – though rather invasive – Euphorbia that has green-yellow 'flowers' in spring. Its charm lies more in the dense, fluffy appearance of the leaves which are very soft to the touch. If it outgrows its allotted space it is uncommon enough to be received with pleasure by one's friends, but it has not quite got to this stage here yet. It dies down in winter, leaving a stemmy, rooting tangle.

Euphorbias are a strange family, producing the unlikely Poinsettia that has as near cousins many tall and spiny cacti. *E. robbiae* is a woodland-growing variety, needing deep, rich soil, as does our native wild plant *E. amygdaloides* or Wood Spurge. *E. myrsinites* has glaucous grey-green leaves and likes a baking situation on a rock face, producing interesting yellow 'flowers' in early summer. The gastropods love it as well, so it has been moved for its own safety to the stone trough and is recovering nicely. The gigantic *E. wulfenii* also needs full sun, and as this grows to a handsome height of about five feet (and sometimes more) it should be sited most carefully and with some thought because it cannot be moved once it has settled in and begun to grow. *E. griffithii* 'flowers' in late May producing glowing orange-red bracts at the top of two-foot stems. The colour lasts for some time, but this member of the family shares the invasive habits of many of its brothers and may need to be watched. *E. polychroma* is a lovely thing, having brilliant yellow heads of bracts in early spring. It needs a sunny position and has no character quirks.

At the end of the rockery the frosted stems and leaves of Schizostylis wait to be cleared away. This plant is so clearly happy here that it must stay where it is, and in my daily journeys up and down the path I can see its pink stars opening almost every day during the darkest months of the year. Beyond the ever-increasing patch of Schizostylis the brown soil is broken by some tightly curled fernlike leaves that are just beginning to emerge. These belong to the charming Sweet Cicely (*Myrrhis odorata*) whose leaves are the first among the umbellifers to appear in spring. For Sweet Cicely it is spring already, though the old year has not ended.

The turning circle of the garden year sometimes revolves all too quickly and sometimes slows almost to a standstill: the circle is like a coronet, gemmed at all times with jewels of different lustres and different colours, but all of them equally precious. One that is beloved all over the temperate world is the Primrose, and in the thin bright December sun, many of the clumps beneath the apple tree on the lawn are already in flower. They are one tone with the pale sunlight, but their wide-open flowers mean that spring has come early to the cottage garden.

Tabitha on the path to the studio

Index

Bold page references refer to illustrations

Aconitum anglicum **46**, 49, **51**
Adiantum capillus veneris 128
Aegopodium podagraria 90
Agapanthus 90, **91**
Akebia quinata **36**, 42
Algerian Iris 20, **20**, 21
Allium 96
Anemone blanda 30, **31**
coronaria De Caen **28**, 30, **30**
pulsatilla 39, **40**
Angelica 56
Angelica archangelica 56
Angel's Fishing Rods **75**, 76
Apple **99**, **141**
'Keswick Codlin' 12
Aquilegia vulgaris **46**, 47
Arum Lily **7**, 26
Asparagus sprengeri 16
Asplenium scolopendrium 128
Aucuba japonica 136
Autumn Snowflake 12

Barley 98
Bay 32
Bean 94, **107**
Bear's Foot 10, **13**
Bindweed 66, 70, 71, 72
Bishop Weed 90
Blackberries 98
Bluebell 36, **36**, **39**
Bougainvillea 22, 86
Bracken **133**
Broad Bean **101**
Broad Buckler Fern 132
Broad-leaved Willow Herb 76
Buddleia **78**, **80**

Calendula officinalis 56, **57**, 103
Calystegia sepium 66, 70, 71, 72
Campanula medium 67, **70**
Candytuft 36
Canterbury Bells 67, **70**
Carrot 94, **95**
Cathedral Bells 74
Chamaepericlymenum canadensis 112, **117**
Cherry Laurel 41, **41**
Chimonanthus fragrans (Praecox) 20, **20**, **23**, 136
Chinese Lanterns 110
Choisya ternata 103
Christmas Rose **151**
Chrysanthemum 'Balcombe Perfection' **125**, 133
maximum **76**, 77
Cistus ladanifer 70

Citrullus colocynthus 23, 24
Citrus sinensis **22**, **22**, 29
Clematis macropetala 'Blue Lagoon' 42, **43**
orientalis 'Lemon Peel' **66**, **93**, 94
'Lasurstern' 58
'Ville de Lyon' 58, **59**
Cnicus benedictus 23, 24
Cobaea scandens 74
Colletia armata 136
Coloquintida 23, 24
Coltsfoot 27, **27**
Common Polypody **122**, **126**, 128, **129**
Corkscrew hazel 15, **17**
Corncockle 37, 38, 68
Cornflowers 38, **71**
Cornus alba 'Elegantissima' 8, 18
canadensis, now *chamaepericlymenum canadensis* 112, **117**
florida 116
kousa 52, 116
sanguinea 117, **119**
Corylus avellana contorta 15, **17**
Cosmea **78**, 87, **89**
Cotoneaster horizontalis 132
Crocus 15, 21, **21**
Crown Imperial 32, **33**
Cyclamen coum 15, **16**, 84
neapolitanum 84
persicum 86
Cymbidium 22, **24**
Cynara scolymus 37
Cypress **153**

Dahlia **92**, 104, **105**
Daisies 9
Dandelion 44
Daphne 18, 28, **28**, **29**
Delphinium 55, **57**
Dianthus gratianopolitanus 65
barbatus 67, **67**
Diarama pulcherrimum **75**, 76
Dog Rose **109**
Dogwood 117, **119**
Dipsacus fullonum **149**
Dracunculus vulgaris 62
Dragon Arum 62
Dryopteris dilatata 132
Dryopteris felix-mas 128

Eleagnus pungens 136
Elecampane 81, **81**, 82
Epilobium montanum 76
Eranthis hyemalis 14, 15
Erythronium tuolumnense 'Pagoda' 32, 42
Euphorbia amygdaloides 156

cyparissias 156
griffithii 156
myrsinites 156
polychroma 156
pulcherrima 152, 156
robbiae 156
wulfenii 156
Evening Primrose 67

Fig **103**, **110**
Fox & Cubs 68
Fuchsia 'Little Fellow' **5**

Galanthus 11, 12, **26**
Gardener's Garters 72, **76**
Garlic 96, **97**
Garrya elliptica 18, 19
Geranium 54
Geum urbanum 65
Gingko biloba **108**, 112
Globe Artichoke 37
Glory Vine **112–113**, 114
Grannybonnets **46**, 47
Grass **86**, **87**
Ground Elder 90
Ground Ivy 46, **47**
Guelder Rose 114, **116**

Hamamelis mollis 12, **14**
Hard Shield Fern **129**, 132
Hart's Tongue Fern 128
Hazel **28**, 34
Hedera helix **138**, **144–145**, 145
canariensis 'variegata' Gloire de Marengo **8**, 71, 145, **146**
conglomerata 147
dentata 'Aurea' 148
Goldheart 147
Green Ripple 147
Sagittaefolia 147
Silver Queen syn. 'Marginata' 148
Hedychium gardnerianum 78, **85**, 86
Helianthus annua 82
Helleborus atrorubens 9
foetidus 10, **13**
niger 10, **151**
orientalis 8, 9, 10, 28
Hemerocallis dumortierii 38
Heuchera 154
Hips **108**, **109**, **120**
Holly **142**, **143**, 148
Holy Thistle 23, 24
Honesty **44**, 45, 47
Honeysuckle **92**, **100**
Hydrangea 122, **130–131**
Hypericum 42, 60

Iberis sempervirens 36
Inula helenium 81, **81**, 82
Iris chrysographes 55
foetidissima **122**, **135**
pseudacorus 37, 64
sibirica 55, **55**
unguicularis **20**, 20, 21
xiphioides 38
Ivy **138**, **144–145**

Jasminum nudiflorum 142, **142**, 147

Laburnum × *vossii* 28, 44
Lamiastrum galeobdolon 'Variegatum' 153
Lamium album 52, **53**
Laurus nobilis 32
Lavender **78**, 80
Lavandula spica **78**, 80
Lilac 52, **53**
Lily of the Valley 47, **50**
Lungwort 28, **29**, 34
Leek **95**, 96
Lesser Celandine **34**, 35
Lettuce 96, **96**
Leucojum 11, 12
Lilium candidum 69
pyrenaicum **77**
Royal Gold **69**
Lily of the Valley **50**
Lonicera 'Brownii' **92**, **100**
periclymenum 68
Lungwort 28, **29**
Lychnis coronaria 62, **63**
githago 37, 38

Madonna Lily 69
Magnolia lilliflora Nigra 41
sieboldii 41
soulangeana 41
stellata 41
Mahonia japonica **25**, 27, 140
Maidenhair Fern 128
Male Fern 128
Mandragora officinarum 28
Mandrake 28
Marguerites 76
Marigold 56, **57**, 103
Matteuccia struthiopteris 132
Mistletoe 142, **155**
Monkshood **46**, 49, **51**
Morning Glory 40, 70
Moss **148**
Mulberry **98**, 101
Myrrhis odorata 156
Myrtle 102, **104**
Myrtus communis 102, **104**

Nasturtium **66**, 82, 88
Narcissus poeticus Actaea **36**, 40
pseudonarcissus 23, **28**
White Lion 38
Nerine 124, **127**

Oak **111**
Oats 98
Oenothera biennis 67
Onion 96, **97**

Opium Poppy **65**, 74
Orange 22, **22**, 29
Osmunda regalis 132
Ostrich-Feather Fern 132
Oxalis 82
Oxlips 30

Paeonia mascula 48, **48**
Pansy 52, **66**
Papaver somniferum **65**, 74
Parrotia persica **123**, 124
Parthenocissus quinquefolia syn. *Vitis hederacea* **108**, 114, **115**
henryana 114
Pasque Flower 39, **40**
Passiflora caerulea 101
Constance Elliott 101
Passion Flower 101
Peach **20**, 102
Peas 96, **102**
Pelargonium 26, 78, 79
Mrs Henry Cox **79**
Paul Crampel **83**
Peonies 48, 48, 108
Periwinkles 10, **11**, 136
Petasites fragrans 19, **19**
Phalaris arundinacea variegata 72, **77**
Physalis franchetii 110
Physocarpus opulifolius luteus 38
Pilosella aurantiacum 68
Pinks **62**, 64, 65
Plantago 140
Plantains 140
Poinsettia 152, 156
Polygonatum baldschuanicum 146
Polypodium vulgare **122**, **126**, 128, **129**
Polystichium aculeatum **129**, 132
Polystichium setiferum densum 128
Potato 96, **97**
Prunus laurocerasus 41, **41**
pissardii 10, 136
lusitanica 41
Pulmonaria officinalis 28, **29**, 34
Purple Deadnettle **32**
Pyrenean Lily **77**

Radish 94, **94**
Rose Campion 62, **63**
Roses: Apothecary's Rose 64
R. canina **54**
Guinee **65**
Harry Wheatcroft 58
Ispahan 64
Joseph's Coat 58
R. longicuspis 46
Mermaid 68, **68**
Nevada 54
Rosa Mundi 58, 59
R. rubiginosa 60
William Lobb 64
Zambra **55**
Rose Hips: *R. canina* **108**, **109**
Cupid 111, **120**
Frau Dagmar Hastrup 111
R. moyesii 111
Nevada 111
R. rubrifolia 111
Romneya 81
Royal Fern 132
Rubus ulmifolius bellidiflorus 88
Russian Vine 146
Rye **3**, **86**, **87**, 98

Schizostylis coccinea 119
Scots Pine **150**
Sempervivums 154
Skimmia 40
Sloe **122**, **139**
Snake's Head Fritillary 37, **39**
Snowdrop 11, 12, **26**
Spring Snowflakes 11, 12
Spurge Laurel 28, **29**
Steep Holm Peony 48, 48
Summer Snowflake 12
Sunflower 82
Sweet Cicely 156
Sweet Violet **36**, 42
Sweet William 67, **67**
Sweet Woodruff 48
Syringa 52, **53**

Taraxacum officinale 44
Teasel **149**
Thyme **60**
Tradescantia virginiana 92
Tulips **1**, 29, 32
Tussilago farfara 27, **27**

Viburnum bodnantense Dawn **134**, 136
opulus 114, 116, **116**
tomentosum mariesii 50, 116
Vincas 10, **11**, 136
Viola odorata **36**, 42
Virginia Creeper **108**, 114, **115**
Viscum album **142**, **155**
Vitis coignetiae **112–113**, 114

Wand Flower **74**, 77
Wallflowers **37**, 42, 67
White Deadnettle 52, **53**
Wild Daffodils 23, **28**
Wild Honeysuckle 68
Winter Aconite 14, 15
Winter Heliotrope 19, **19**
Winter Jasmine 142, **142**, **147**
Wintersweet 20, **20**, **23**, 136
Witch Hazel 12, **14**
Wood Avens 65

Yellow Archangel 153

Zantedeschia aethiopica **7**, 26